Breathing New Life

Finding Happiness after Tragedy

Breathing New Life

Finding Happiness after Tragedy

Bunny Leach

atmosphere press

Dedicated to
All Who Believe that Happiness is A Choice

TABLE OF CONTENTS

INTRODUCTION

Oh, the places you'll go!
—Dr. Seuss

Welcome to my second book in a three-part series. The first book, *Letting Nicki Go: A Mother's Journey Through Her Daughter's Cancer,* published in 2019, is a memoir that tells the story of my teenage daughter's three-year battle with a glioblastoma: the deadliest brain tumor with no cure. The years after my daughter's death were spent searching for answers: chiefly, *why?* I spoke with God often, and, though he comforted me, no answers came. For me there is no answer, only acceptance; and when I stopped searching, I eventually learned to breathe new life.

Breathing New Life: Finding Happiness after Tragedy continues my story of hope. As I grieved my daughter's death, God eventually brought me blessings through her tragedy. Seven years after my daughter died, I experienced an unusual turn of events that helped me to breathe new life. The story didn't end with one book—and now I want to share the rest of the story of new beginnings. When God took my beloved daughter from me to be with him, I had no idea that he was going to send me someone special to spend the rest of my life with—and this unlikely turn of events in my life led me to believe that my future was predetermined by God. He was working on my behalf but I didn't know it at the time, as I was consumed in my own pain. But ultimately, through tragedy and with time I learned the depths of what trusting God means.

I encourage you to choose happiness, dream big, and

always pray and trust God—because dreams really do come true, and miracles happen.

Preface
A TIME TO DREAM

My daughter, Nicki, died from brain cancer fourteen years ago. She was nineteen when she took her last breath.

We were gathered around her when she died: her father and I, and her brother, Jesse, who placed his hand over his sister's heart until its last beat. In the moment when she took her last breath, Jesse captured something very precious and intimate—something that belongs to him alone and will stay with him forever: his little sister's final heartbeat.

I don't think that grieving ever completely ends when you lose someone you love dearly, especially when it's your child. What I've learned through my pain and suffering, though, is that life continues even if it feels like life has stopped, as it felt for me when my daughter died. I had to find a new path to happiness, and eventually, with time, I did. New people came into my life and helped me heal; I learned how to adapt to the many changes that came after Nicki died. My life had changed drastically after her death, and I had to accept changes that, at first, I resisted; finally, though, I came to a point of acceptance. She died and I wanted to make something beautiful out of her death. I'm thankful that I had her for nineteen years, and believe that she came for a reason: she taught me how to trust God.

I'm still sad that she's not here with me anymore, and I know that the pain will never go away. There is sadness when I see other mothers and daughters having lunch together, or shopping together, and I know that I will never do those things with her anymore. And when I think about how much she suffered at such a young age I want to hide my face and cry. But I hold on to our memories—both happy and sad—because in life she experienced both. And now, so do I.

While battling cancer, Nicki gained knowledge beyond her teenage years, in fact so much so that her knowledge seemed to come from someone much older. There were times when I felt that she was the mother and I was the daughter. For instance, I will never forget the morning after Nicki's pediatric neurosurgeon at the University of Florida in Gainsville, Dr. Pincus, came into her hospital room and sat beside her bed. He had performed a twenty-hour surgery on her brain the night before, a very delicate surgery to remove the cancer without taking her healthy brain tissue. Brain surgeons are skilled and meticulous with their instruments and their hands—I thanked God for that.

On that morning, he came to her hospital room in the ICU to give us the results of the tumor biopsy. At this point we didn't know what kind of brain cancer she had. Regrettably, he was unable to give us the news we had all prayed for, but while sitting in a chair that he pulled up close beside Nicki's bed, and while looking directly into her eyes, he spoke in a calm and sensitive tone. Carefully and graciously he explained to her that the tumor was a stage four glioblastoma: the fastest and most aggressive brain cancer there is.

After he delivered the sad news to her, she asked him this: "How long do I have?"

It was hard to hear a sixteen-year-old girl ask him such a pointed question, especially after we had prayed so long for a miracle. Given the severity of her disease he answered her gently but truthfully while looking steadily into her pretty blue eyes.

"One to three years, Nicki. But then—I am not God."

He dropped his head in sadness. Her doctor was a wise man, and left her fate in the hands of God. That was comforting for me, and I hoped it was for her too.

When Nicki was released to come home from the hospital, she had gained even more wisdom and spoke even wiser words that have stayed with me ever since. One evening, as we were relaxing on the couch in the living room of our beach house, she looked me in the eye the same way she looked at Dr. Pincus that day in the ICU.

"I've always wondered what my thing would be," she said.

Thinking back on this, I didn't know at the time what she meant by "my thing." It wasn't until months after she died when I figured out what she meant: "her thing" was what would end her life. I guess at the time I wouldn't let my mind go there or think about that. But, ironically, after she died "her thing" became *my* thing too—which was the fear of how I would survive without her. There is no doubt in my mind that both of our concerns centered on our love for each other, and that caused us to think about how the other one would survive if the other were to die. We had lived and loved nineteen years as mother and daughter; it was inevitable that survival for either of us without the other would be hard. It's something you don't want to think about until you are told that you have cancer and there is no cure.

The three years that she battled cancer should have

been the best years of her life: she was young, a teenager. In fact, she had just obtained her driver's license when she began having seizures and we had no choice but to take her driving privileges away. She should have been healthy and vibrant and growing her independence at sixteen, just like her friends and classmates were doing. She should have been thinking about what college she might like to attend in the future, and having sleepovers, and going to parties with her friends.

Instead of planning, though, she was preparing—and not for her future, but for her death. Nicki wasn't in control of how much time she had; instead the tumor controlled everything in her life. Most of her time was spent in the hospital or the clinic receiving chemotherapy and brain radiation, as well as going to regular doctor appointments, receiving CT scans and MRIs, and enduring long stays in the hospital. And, perhaps expectedly, the many doctor visits and hospital stays caused her to become estranged from some of her classmates and friends. At a time when she needed her peers more than ever, she was too sick and tired from the cancer treatments to keep up with them—for although her classmates and friends were very attentive to her and visited her often, they had commitments to school, work, and jobs. They tried to come see her every opportunity they had, though, and that made her so happy.

After Nicki died I felt a huge void, especially when I transitioned from being her mother to becoming the mother who lost a child. Even worse: I became the pitied mother. I felt that I had been branded without my permission. People felt sorry for me and I understood why—how could they not? But it was uncomfortable to know that when people saw me, or thought about me, it made them sad. I just wanted to be invisible to alleviate their discomfort. My close friends, though, were not in this group: they comforted me, held me with love, and cried with me.

Thankfully, grieving subsides somewhat with time and the pain isn't as raw. People eventually go about their lives as if nothing happened. It is comforting to know that life becomes a bit more normal with time. Watching Nicki overcome all the challenges she dealt with while battling brain cancer taught me to be strong and brave like she was. Perhaps while she was sick she was teaching me and providing me with some of her strength because she knew I would need it. Her mental and physical strength was truly something to behold.

At her funeral in our church, Nicki's friend Ryan gave the eulogy, and in closing he read a touching letter that Nicki had sent to him just weeks before she died. She closed the letter with a paraphrase of a quote from Dr. Seuss, one of her favorite authors: "Don't frown because it's over... smile because it happened."

The choice was mine: how would I choose to live without her? I could choose to be happy or I could choose to stay sad, which I knew wouldn't honor her at all. It didn't take me long to decide which path to take, because Nicki was my teacher and I want to be like her: I chose to be happy. I knew Nicki would want that for me because she chose happiness even while fighting for her life.

Before Nicki died she gave me an assignment: "Find a way to help others" who were going through the same thing as she was.

"You see how it is, Mommy—you can do something to

help," she told me.

As I continue to move forward with my life, I want to keep my daughter's memory alive both through my writing, and through the Nicki Leach Foundation: a non-profit organization created in 2006 in her memory. The Nicki Leach Foundation helps young adults with cancer by giving them modest financial grants so that they can continue to pursue their educational dreams and goals. And in addition to its educational work, the Foundation also provides funding for glioblastoma research in adolescents and young adults.

Nicki helped me to be a survivor, and, with God's grace and mercy, I will go forward and do everything I can to keep her legacy alive and to help others diagnosed with cancer.

SEAWALK

The summer of 1991 was hot and humid in North Florida, especially on the day my realtor took me to see a house for sale in Ponte Vedra Beach. The beach house was the first of four houses that she was taking me to look at that day, but even before seeing it I had already developed a strong desire to buy it based on its location; the house was just two miles from my husband Mike's new job as tennis director at the Ponte Vedra Inn and Club, a five-star, five-diamond beachfront resort. Our family was moving from Atlanta, Georgia, to Florida because Mike had recently retired from competing on the ATP tour, the Association of Tennis Professionals men's tennis tour. During this time the kids and I had accompanied him for five years traveling across the United States, Europe, Asia, Australia, and South Africa while he competed in tournaments to make a living for our young family. It was while we were traveling together on the tour that I became pregnant with our first child, Jesse; Nicki was born twenty-two months after Jesse.

My husband and I had made the decision early on that when the kids became of school age he would retire from the tour and we would find a permanent place for our family to live, as at some point our two kids would need to have a more stable life than constant international travel and living out of hotels. So, naturally, we were all excited as a family when he accepted the job as director of tennis at the Ponte Vedra Inn and Club. It was perfect timing: Jesse was in third grade and Nicki was in first grade, so they would grow up at the beach and make wonderful friendships from a young age.

We were even happier when we learned that we would have full member privileges to all the amenities at the club. The Inn and Club, as it's called by the locals, has many unique amenities. There are two spectacular golf courses, two large swimming pools, and a large gym with views overlooking the Atlantic Ocean, along with a luxury day spa, three upscale restaurants, and several coastal-themed retail shops. If we lived just two miles from the Inn and Club it would be so convenient for the kids and me to go back and forth several times a day to play tennis—especially since I played on tennis leagues when we lived in Atlanta and was a member of the Atlanta Lawn and Tennis association, one of the world's largest woman's tennis association leagues. As a member of the Inn and Club I could join the woman's tennis league there; the kids could play and compete in junior USTA tennis, and could join the swim team. We could ride our bikes, or even walk, to the club and back since it was just two miles away.

The beach house I was interested in was just a half mile off Ponte Vedra Boulevard—where the Inn and Club was located. I liked that the house had a private road that dead-ended into Coastal Oak Circle; the Circle is surrounded with views of protected Florida Guana preserve land, wildlife, and a tributary that flows under the road and connects to several lakes surrounding the other homes on the Circle.

So, when my realtor pulled up in front of the Coastal Oak Circle house for the first time, I became even more intrigued. My first impression was *I want this house*. There was a large window in the front of the house and an old oak tree in front of the window that leaned to one side; I was intrigued by the tree, and thought it was a work of art. The leaning oak tree was on the right side of a long and winding sandstone sidewalk leading to the front door of the house, making me think of how Dorothy must have felt when she saw the yellow brick road for the first time.

When my realtor parked her car in the driveway, we got out of the car and walked the sidewalk leading to the front entry of the house; she unlocked the door and held it open, and I stepped inside. My eyes went right through the house to the view of the back porch and then through the floor-to-ceiling windows where I saw a spectacular view of the lake and the surrounding Guana preserve. I also saw several large turtles sunning themselves along the edge of the lake, and some white and gray water birds, and a single alligator swimming in the lake. I loved the view of the back yard: it looked like a colorful painting. I hadn't even looked at the inside of the house and I'd already fallen in love with the view. I thought about how soothing it would be to look at the lake surrounded with natural preserve land every day while writing. Right then and there I knew in my heart that this was the house for our family. As I stood looking out the front window toward the oak tree I was filled with excitement. Then my realtor reminded me that the house also came with private beach access—everything just kept getting better and better.

Another perk that came with the house that I loved was that no one had lived in it because it was a new build: in fact, it was the builders' model home. This sealed the deal for me; I felt right then and there that the house was built specifically for our family of four.

So, I said yes. And then it was ours.

WHEN LIFE DOESN'T MAKE SENSE

2002

It was Nicki's sophomore year at Douglas Anderson School of the Arts. She was so happy that she had been cast in the school production of *Once Upon a Mattress*, and even happier when Dr. Lee Beger, the Chair of Theatre at the school, announced to the cast and crew that they had been selected to perform at Tallahassee's performing arts center, Theatre Tallahassee. This was a big honor, not only for the school but particularly for the theater department and its students. Being selected to perform at state was a huge honor because many other schools all over Florida had competed for this opportunity—and not all had been chosen to perform.

The kids had worked very hard for this chance, so naturally they were extremely excited to have succeeded. During the trip, the theater students and the orchestra would travel together and stay in a hotel in Tallahassee; once there, they would perform to much larger audiences than they were accustomed to. I was a chaperone for the trip and roomed with another chaperone, the mother of one of Nicki's friends.

On the day of their big performance in Tallahassee, Nicki didn't show up for the morning rehearsal, upsetting Dr. Beger who thought Nicki was being irresponsible—even though we all knew that wasn't Nicki's nature. I was sitting in the auditorium and the student actors were in costume on stage ready to start rehearsal, but Nicki wasn't there with them. Everyone was confused, turning to one another and asking if they knew where she was, but no one had an answer.

I was deeply concerned: Nicki had been on cloud nine to be performing at state and would never have missed the show; she loved acting and performing too much, so I knew something must have happened. And, I knew that she would also never want to disappoint Dr. Beger—she loved "Doc," as the kids called her. I knew this couldn't be on purpose... so, where was she? I was extremely worried!

I got up from my seat and went to her hotel room to see what had happened, but when I knocked on her door no one answered. I became scared; this was not like Nicki. At the same time, a few of the students left the theater and went out looking for her. Someone eventually found her roommate—a girl who was part of the tech crew—and asked her if she knew where Nicki was. She told us that when she'd left the room that morning, Nicki had still been sleeping. We were all getting more worried so we asked her roommate to go back to the room and see if Nicki was there. And, to our surprise and even greater concern, there she was: in her bed, still sound asleep.

This didn't seem right to me. When her roommate woke Nicki, she immediately dressed and made her way to the stage for rehearsal. Once she was there, Dr. Beger expressed her disappointment for Nicki not being more responsible, and in the face of her mentor's disappointment, Nicki started crying. I felt awful and perplexed about the situation: it seemed very odd for her to not have heard her alarm. I was nervous and confused—I had no idea what was going on.

That evening the cast performed the show in front of a packed theater, and during the performance Nicki seemed fine: she was animated and happy; she remembered all her lines. And the Saturday evening show and the Sunday matinee were exactly the same. After the matinee, the kids packed up, loaded the busses, and headed back to Jacksonville. Everyone was bushed after the weekend. Nicki sat in the seat beside me and, with her head on my lap, slept the whole way home.

When we got home I asked her what happened on Friday morning when she didn't show up to rehearsal on time. She said that she had set her alarm, but didn't hear it, apparently in such a deep sleep—due to the tumor, we would realize later—that the alarm didn't wake her up. It was another of the many signs that something was wrong, but we didn't realize it. At this point, we just didn't know what was going on.

Then, on October 3—the morning of Nicki's seventeenth birthday—things became even stranger. Her classmates had planned a birthday party for her, which was going to take place during their acting class. When she found out about the party she could hardly wait to go to school and celebrate with her friends. But when she awoke the morning of her birthday, she wasn't feeling well, and her excitement for the party dampened. It was evident that the mysterious sleeping patterns and sudden headaches she'd been complaining of for the past few months had gotten worse. And now, the timing was horrible.

Even though she seemed all right when she went to bed the night before, she was far from all right when she woke up the morning of her birthday. Not only was she sick, but she seemed mentally confused and had an excruciating headache. I wondered what in the world could have happened overnight that would make her so confused?

I had expected her to wake up well rested and excited to go to school to celebrate with her classmates. Her classmates had let me know weeks ahead of time that they would be decorating the theater department with balloons and other party favors in her honor; they had also put a skit together to perform, baked a cake, and had presents as well. Her classmates had known Nicki hadn't been feeling well for a while, so they wanted her birthday to include some special surprises.

It wasn't meant to be, though: when Nicki walked into the kitchen the morning of her party, I could tell that something was very wrong. The mysterious illness that had been haunting us for months was turning into a nightmare. None of us could put our finger on what was causing her mental confusion and overall sickness. She didn't have a fever, or any idea of what might be making her sick; she hardly had any energy left in her and, as hard as she tried, she couldn't concentrate; and even though she was sleeping more than she ever had in her life, she would wake fatigued.

But because Nicki was a fighter, she went to school even though she wasn't feeling well. She wouldn't miss her party for anything, and she would never let her friends down after they put it all together for her. That was our Nicki.

While she was at school I worried about her even more. I had raised her for seventeen years; I was her mother, and knew this was something serious—but *what*? It was obvious that something was horribly wrong with my child. Her previous sixteen years had been full of laughter and nonstop energy. I couldn't believe this change in her could just be chalked up to adolescence. There were times recently when Nicki came home from school incredibly upset because she suddenly had to try so hard to keep up with her peers—when previously she'd always had more energy than most of her friends. And then, on Nicki's birthday, her best friend Katie wrote in a card that she didn't think that Nicki liked her anymore and seemed distant. Nicki was crushed by the birthday card, crying over it. I thought, *what is going on?*

Her teachers also sensed something wasn't right: her grades, once all As, had fallen to Cs with no explanation—and poor Nicki had no answer because there was just no known reason. The questions and concerns from her friends and teachers just seemed to hurt and confuse her even more, and they confused and hurt me too. Everyone cared about her and wanted to be helpful, but no one knew how, much less what was causing her symptoms.

This was a time in any teenager's life to begin gaining more freedom—but instead it seemed that Nicki was losing hers. Because of all the strange things that were happening to her I wasn't comfortable with her being away from me, at least not until we figured out what was going on. But on the day of her birthday she insisted that she was going to school and, though I was worried, I allowed it—so she got in her car and drove off. I didn't want to be overprotective and stop her, so I remained content with praying for her as I watched her pull away.

Nicki's high school, Douglas Anderson School of the Arts, is in downtown Jacksonville, fifteen miles away from our house at the beach. After she left, even though I was praying, my mind began to race like it always did when she was out of my sight. At this point I honestly didn't know if she should be driving. I thought about my role as a stay-at-home mom. Nicki and her older brother Jesse were the light of my life; I knew them both like the back of my hand. But during all the confusion about Nicki's mysterious illness I didn't know what to do or where to go for help.

I searched my mind for answers and wondered if something could have happened to her when she was a little girl that might have caused this. Was there something from the past that I missed? But how could I have missed anything? When she was an infant and then a toddler she received all her required immunizations. I took her to the doctor every time she got sick: she'd had ear infections, several rounds of strep throat, and I'm sure she had a virus or two, but she always recovered. I thought back over the years, racking my brain for anything unusual, but I couldn't come up with anything. So, what was it? What was I *missing*?

The mysterious illness had started subtly and progressed slowly during her sophomore year of high school. That's when her health began to quietly decline, and her grades began to gradually drop. So, what was causing this? She always studied and took her schoolwork very seriously. It was heartbreaking to watch her as she struggled to keep up with her class because she couldn't concentrate or retain what she had studied. And it was even harder to watch her having trouble memorizing her lines for theater class—her greatest love. As a child and in middle school she performed in several theater productions and never had a problem with memorization; she always had a fantastic memory. So what was going *on*?

I had already taken her to a handful of doctors, but they weren't yet able to diagnose the cause of her illness. We also paid regular visits to our family practitioner, but he seemed to be searching for answers just like we were. His best idea was that it was a virus—and then he sent us home. One of her doctors thought her symptoms could be from hormonal changes, but I didn't agree: all teenagers go through hormonal changes, but hers were definitely not normal; they were peculiar, unlike anything I'd ever seen or heard of. Everyone who knew her could see the drastic difference in her personality, and expressed their concern. My baby girl, as I called her, had always been upbeat and was extremely bright. She had changed, and we all longed to have our happy, bubbly Nicki back.

The summer before her junior year, her symptoms got even worse. She was constantly fatigued, sleeping all day and night, and this sudden change caused her even more distress. She was scared because she couldn't control anything that was happening to her. One day, she came home from school and told me that one of her best friends had pulled her aside to ask if she were doing drugs. This hurt her so badly: she couldn't believe her close friend would think that. The question hurt me too. *What in the world was going on?*

Having to watch my daughter change from a healthy, robust girl who once had so much energy into a very sick girl who was vomiting, plagued with constant headaches, and had no energy, all at just seventeen years of age, was frightening. But most of all it was heartbreaking: for Nicki, for our entire family, and for her many friends. All I could do was watch her carefully and keep searching for answers.

One day, I went to my closet and took her baby box down from the shelf to search through my journal entries and her baby books. I was looking for any clues that I might have missed back in her infancy, but I couldn't find anything except ear infections—normal for a child. Nor did she have any strange illnesses growing up; in fact, quite the contrary: Nicki was always a happy, healthy baby. I sat for hours, reading through six years of journals all the way from 1985 to 1991. As I did, I saw a picture of my daughter emerge: not only was she smart, but she was athletic like her dad. She began pre-ballet at two, then later danced tap, then added jazz, continuing to dance until high school. She was so full of energy; when her brother took karate lessons, she wanted to as well. Her father began teaching her how to hit tennis balls as early as two years old: he would toss tennis balls to her and she would catch them in her little hands. Since the kids and I had traveled with Mike while he competed on the men's ATP professional tennis tour, she was quite familiar with tennis, and competed in tournaments as a young girl.

But performing arts had become Nicki's real passion. As early as three years old she would act out characters in Disney movies, memorizing and reciting line after line, and singing the lyrics to all her favorite Disney songs. She watched plays and musicals repeatedly without ever tiring, and her love for theater continued to grow stronger every year. Her ultimate dream was to one day perform on Broadway, and when she was in grade school, she landed her first role in community theater as young Molly in *Little Women*. To complement her acting skills, she began voice lessons when she was ten, and when she joined the children's choir at our church, she quickly advanced from singing in the youth church to singing with the adult choir for the Sunday worship services. When she was in middle school she performed in the all-girls show group Believing

Let Us See Him, or BLUSH, a group of five girls led by her voice teacher, Priscilla Johnson. Nicki was the mezzo-soprano in the group, and everyone who heard Nicki sing commented on how her spellbinding voice matched her personality.

Nicki sang her first solo in church when she was in fifth grade. And, ironically, she performed her final vocal solo in the same church, on the same stage, at seventeen, just two days before she was diagnosed with a malignant brain tumor. This was when we finally got our answer to what was causing Nicki to change so drastically right before our very eyes: it was a malignant brain tumor that was hiding undetected in her head, and had been causing her to vomit, and to have horrible headaches and confusion.

The mystery was solved.

This was the turning point in Nicki's life, and in the lives of all who knew her. It was our darkest hour when Nicki was diagnosed with a stage-four brain tumor, a glioblastoma. She had the deadliest brain cancer of all, for which there was, and still is, no cure. The tumor had been hiding in her brain for months—maybe even years—and we hadn't known it.

We had expected her doctors to check for these things, but not a single doctor took an MRI of her brain until she became so sick that her dad and I drove her to Wolfson Children's Hospital in downtown Jacksonville. When we entered through the door of the emergency room, with Nicki dangling from her father's arms like a rag doll, the triage nurse jumped from her seat behind the desk, grabbed a wheel chair, and in just a few moments Nicki was taken to have a CT scan of her brain.

We were devastated! It had never occurred to me, not

in a million years, that this mystery illness might be cancer. And her doctors must not have suspected it either, as not one of them did any tests. When the doctor told us the results of the CT scan, my heart almost stopped beating. I dropped to the floor in shock, but then got up because I knew I had to be strong for her. She would need me even more when we gave Nicki the diagnosis.

Perhaps I was wrong not to suspect cancer was the culprit—maybe her symptoms should have been obvious to me from the start. But I didn't know the symptoms of a brain tumor, so how would I suspect something that deadly? I probably should have suspected it was cancer because it had already taken the lives of many of my family members: my dad had colon cancer and died when he was forty-nine; my grandparents died from cancer in their eighties. But not one of my family members that I know of had a brain tumor. I've since been told by doctors that brain cancer and colon cancer are related somehow, so perhaps there's a genetic link. Some cancers are sneaky and masquerade as other things. I sometimes wonder if Nicki ever thought that she had cancer but didn't say it? I don't know the answer, but we had always relied on her doctors to check for everything if her symptoms pointed in that direction.

I was in shock when we found out that she had a malignant brain tumor. At that moment in time I felt so sad for her and vowed to not let cancer steal her dream to move to New York City and pursue her passion to perform on Broadway. She had so many goals and dreams for her life, and she was such a beautiful young woman, and in the end, she never let cancer steal her goals: she wanted to graduate from high school—and so she did; then she wanted to go to college, and eventually completed that goal, attending college for a short time before she died.

It broke my heart to watch her struggle to achieve her goals, and it was hard to accept that it was cancer that robbed her of her dream, shattered her passion, and stole her chance to move to New York City and make her dream come true. Cancer interfered with everything she needed to make her dream come true: her balance, her speech, her eyesight, and her memory were all eventually affected because of the tumor. Toward the end of her life, Nicki's memory was so bad that she couldn't remember what her favorite foods were. It was devastating.

But all the while she remained strong and brave throughout the journey, continuing to fight for her life. She never gave up. I witnessed her courage and her strength every day. Even though she was weak, she would not let anyone keep her from walking with her high school class at graduation. And after graduating, she enrolled at the University of North Florida in Jacksonville. She had always wanted to go away to college closer to New York City, but the necessary cancer treatments meant she needed to stay close to home.

She was disappointed, of course, because her desire had always been to go out of state to a performing arts college to pursue acting. She fought through two semesters of college, making us incredibly proud of her resilience. The entire time that Nicki battled cancer, her hard work ethic and her determination to never give up were evident to everyone who knew her.

I'm happy to say that cancer lost in the end, because it could never steal Nicki's beauty, charm, or her grace. And it will never be able to steal her legacy either. She was truly beautiful from the inside out. Her fun-loving personality and her giddy laughter were gifts that she shared with others; through the whole journey, her gifts shone brighter than ever. She never stopped smiling, not even in the end.

For her last Christmas, her paternal grandparents gave her a camera as a gift, and though she had already lost sight in one eye, she used her other eye to capture lovely images. We watched her creative endeavors blossom as the camera became her constant companion, a tool for photographing her favorite things with the time she had left: pictures of the Atlantic Ocean where she used to walk, pray, and collect shells; landscapes and shots of local wildlife—water birds and turtles; personal photos of her friends and family. These precious photos have now been preserved for a lifetime in books and greeting cards, and her best framed photography has been displayed in public buildings and presented at art shows.

Her strength and perseverance never waned while she took her journey home. At some point during the three years she battled cancer, the tables turned, and she became the teacher, and I became her student.

Nicki took her last breath on April 29, 2005. It was one day short of my own mom's seventieth birthday.

I will forever remember my daughter Nicki as a God-fearing young woman whose passion was in performing arts. A young woman who dreamed of performing on Broadway. Throughout her life she worked hard to develop her natural talents, and she set big goals for herself—though her goals and future dreams were short-lived. As her mother, I believe that her dreams would have eventually been realized here on this earth. Especially her biggest dream of all: Broadway.

Moving forward without her has been a challenge for me. But, taking my lesson from my daughter, I must persevere as she did, continuing my quest to make her dream come true.

MERRY CHRISTMAS, AND HAPPY NEW YEAR

DECEMBER 2004

On December 1, 2004, my husband Mike gathered our family in the living room, where he announced that he would be moving out on January 1 of the new year. After he made this announcement, he went to our bedroom and locked the door behind him, leaving the three of us sitting in our living room.

I didn't know what to say to the kids. I was completely in shock, suddenly heartbroken. At the time, Mike and I had been married for twenty-five years. Even though over the last two years watching Nicki suffer had been incredibly emotionally hard on him, it had been equally hard on all of us as well, and I thought his timing to move out of our house was selfish. Why was he announcing this right before Christmas? And why, after breaking the news, was he waiting to move out until January? This couldn't possibly be helpful for Nicki while she was fighting for her life—as unnecessary stress is the worst thing for anyone with cancer. And how could he do this to Jesse, his son, and to me? How were we going to live together in the house knowing that in a month he was moving out?

And he gave no reason *why*. It hadn't been easy for any of us to watch Nicki suffer—her seizures, headaches, and memory problems—but she needed support from both her parents, and likewise we three needed him and his help. He must not have cared, though. While both kids cried, and

Nicki begged him to stay, he would not relent. It was a stressful month, and Christmas was sad, because the three of us knew that in just six days their father, and my husband, would be gone.

On New Year's Day 2005, a large moving truck pulled into our driveway; two men entered our house, loaded half of our furniture into the truck, and then drove off. The following day I was served divorce papers.

I didn't know any attorneys and, busy as I was taking care of Nicki, I didn't have time to try to find one on my own. Thankfully, my friend Priscilla helped me, as she knew of an attorney who had helped her neighbor in the past when her husband left her and filed for divorce. After Priscilla gave me all the information to contact him, I met with the attorney to go over everything. It was a dark time in my life, driving back and forth to his office on a regular basis; I didn't like that during these appointments I had to leave Nicki at home alone, as at this point she was having frequent seizures.

I tried to contest the divorce, pleading that Mike shouldn't be able to put me through a divorce while our daughter was dying from brain cancer, but I was told that they couldn't stop him. During the weeks that our attorneys were working out the divorce details, Nicki's tumor started progressing, causing her to be hospitalized. It was only when she went into a coma that we temporarily halted the divorce proceedings.

Nicki died four months after her father moved out and filed for divorce. Thankfully our divorce proceedings were put on hold long enough for us to have a funeral and to bury her. But the divorce proceeding resumed that June, and by August our divorce was final.

I was stunned. He never spoke to me again after the divorce was final, and he never gave me any explanation for the divorce, or reason why he filed while our daughter was dying.

Eighty percent of marriages end in divorce *after* the death of a child, but he filed while she was alive and fighting for her life. I will never understand why he chose to do this while she was sick.

Yet though I was devastated, I think the divorce was harder on our two kids than it was for me, and eventually there came a time when I had to stop searching for answers and accept the things I didn't want to. Everything in my life had spun out of control and I could not stop it. But despite the chaos, I will always remember those who helped Nicki and me during the worst time in our lives. My mom was so caring and traveled all the way from El Paso to stay with us for weeks at a time; she made us dinners and drove us to doctor appointments. My sister and her two girls were supportive, and came from Michigan to visit and spend time with us too. There were so many caring friends in our community and from our church who were always helping to bring us meals and kind gifts.

When we found out that Nicki's tumor wasn't responding to treatment, her big brother Jesse made the choice to leave the University of Miami, where he had earned a full music scholarship, in order to come home and help us through the hardest times we would ever face. Everyone was so proud of Jesse, especially when, a year after Nicki died, he returned to school and graduated *summa cum laude* from the University of North Florida. I don't know what Nicki and I would have done without him.

2005

*The future belongs to those who believe
in the beauty of their dreams.*
—Eleanor Roosevelt

Returning to college wasn't what I had planned for my future—but then, I wasn't in control of much of my life at that point. When Mike moved out and filed for divorce, the court must have believed that since I no longer had Nicki or a husband to take care of, and since Jesse was living on his own, I would need something to do with my time. I had given up my career as a hairdresser in 1981 when we were married so that I could travel and support Mike on the ATP men's professional tennis tour. Five years later, when he retired from the tour, we had two kids and I became a full-time stay-at-home wife and mother from that point on. When the kids became of school age I carpooled and volunteered at their school on a regular basis; and when Nicki was diagnosed with cancer in 2002 I became her primary caretaker. It was a surprise to me, then, that as part of my divorce settlement Mike was ordered to pay for my rehabilitation to go back to college and pursue a new career.

Going back to school right after Nicki died was the furthest thing from my mind, and honestly it was not what I wanted to do at the time. But I was told that I had to pick a course of study right away so that the court could finalize the divorce papers. I guess that's how the system works, but it was almost impossible for me to know what I wanted to major in. Mostly I wanted to get the legal stuff over with and not have to make a major decision right then and there. I wasn't thinking clearly enough to figure anything out: I had just lost my daughter, and then lost my marriage. If I would have been given some time—maybe a year—to think about it, I might have chosen better than I eventually did. It had been a long time since I had been in college, and I knew that going back at my age and with my current state of mind would be challenging: a grieving mind is not a clear mind for learning.

The other problem was that I would be walking the same campus paths as Nicki had. Just the thought of my own return to college brought back the memory of my daughter taking her final walk across campus with her brother. It was her last day at college and Nicki had wanted to walk across campus to the cafeteria to get pizza with Jesse, something they had often done together, but she was so weak that Jesse had to brace her with his strong arms around her waist, almost carrying her. They proceeded to walk together ever so carefully and slowly, step by step, from one end of the university to the other, for her last time on campus.

Whenever I considered attending college myself, my mind immediately would fill with memories of her like that one. When I thought about how brave she was while attending college, I was reminded that I too must be brave—but I wasn't sure if I had the same strength that my daughter had. Yet if I wanted to finalize the divorce, I had to pick a course of study quickly. And since I was being forced to choose a career path so soon after my daughter's death, I chose to study grief counseling.

There is a reason for everything, though. When I returned to college and was immersed in an environment with vibrant young students who were excited about life and their futures, it was hard to face their enthusiasm. The young healthy women on campus were pursuing their dreams and goals at the same time that my daughter had just lost all of hers, and I felt like that loss was being thrown in my face. But after time, I took strength from their excitement, as it helped me to want to be vibrant like they were: the students were so full of motivation, and I hoped that it would rub off on me. I wanted to stop feeling sorry for myself, so it was probably a good thing for me to be around young people. And besides—I didn't have anything else to do. And maybe that was a gift from Nicki: even though I was missing my daughter badly, when I saw the young students on campus I longed to be happy like they were. That was what Nicki would want for me.

The reality is that death and divorce are not a good combination: I had just buried my daughter and my marriage was over; I could barely think clearly about anything. Nevertheless, I enrolled in four psychology classes as part of my grief counseling degree. When I enrolled in a grief counseling degree, I had thought it would help me through my grieving. The problem was, though, I could hardly retain the material from my classes because it hit too close to home and, presented with the experience of loss over and over, I couldn't concentrate. My class on lifespan development was especially hard to sit through without crying because it covered the stages from conception and birth to death.

For the next two years, my mind wandered back

constantly; I was engulfed mentally and emotionally in Nicki's suffering, unable to move forward with my thinking. Things would randomly pop into my mind, surreal memories and snippets of thought, like when I was advised to talk to a hospice grief counselor the day Nicki died. I thought it was the right thing to do at the time, so I made an appointment for a counseling session. I didn't know what to expect because I had never been to grief counseling before and, as it turned out, my first session did not go well. My counselor seemed sleepy while I was talking to her, and after twenty minutes she suddenly fell asleep right in her chair! Maybe she was overworked and tired, but it crushed me, and I never went back. I don't mean to say anything negative about grief counseling as a profession or practice, and in fact I think it's highly important and necessary. But I had a bad experience, and ultimately it wasn't the path I chose to take to recover from my loss. Prayer and meditation worked better for me at the time. I had to trust God to show me the way.

Finally, after two unsuccessful years in college, I realized that I had made a huge mistake in following that career path: I didn't want to spend the rest of my life in a profession that deals primarily with grief. This may seem strange coming from a mother whose teenage daughter died from cancer, but I had to be honest with myself about how I felt. My feelings might change with time, but at that moment I had to find the right direction for me—and grief counseling wasn't my direction.

My Lifespan Development professor must have sensed that I wasn't enjoying my current curriculum. One day after class, she asked me if I would walk across campus with her, as she had something she wanted to talk to me about. Interested in what she had to say, I readily accepted the invitation, gathered my books, and followed her out the door.

"I know that you're grieving your daughter," she said as we walked, "and although I haven't experienced the same heartbreaking loss that you have, I can see you're trying to move forward with your life. You've expressed to me that you want to help people in some way and I thought you might want to explore life coaching. We have a local school here in Jacksonville. I can give you the information if you want to check it out."

I wondered where was this heading, and continued to listen. As we walked, my professor proceeded to tell me about what life coaching is, and what a life coach does.

"Life coaches help people make life transitions," she said. "Coaches are not counselors or therapists, but rather coaches help people move forward and chart a course for success. They help people achieve their intended dreams and goals."

I had spoken with my professor a few times before this conversation, so she knew that I wanted to help people in a positive way, and not just focus on the grieving process. It seems that's why she felt that life coaching seemed to be a better fit for me than grief counseling. As we talked, she stressed that coaching wasn't counseling or therapy, but rather a *relationship* where the coach forms a partnership with their client to guide and encourage success. Plus, coaching doesn't look backward at the past as much as it looks to the future.

"So, what do you think?" she asked.

I paused and thought for a minute. I had an overwhelming feeling that God had led me to her. And, at this point I had gone through three years of bad news and sorrow, and I wanted finally to go forward and honor Nicki.

"Oh, my gosh, coaching sounds like something I would be very interested in," I said.

She smiled. "Great, I'll give you all the information. And by the way—I know the clinical psychologist at the school, so I'll give you his contact information. I think life coaching would be a good fit for you, Bunny, and you can obtain your certification as soon as possible."

I thanked her as she went into her office, and I went away feeling optimistic and somewhat revived.

This was exciting for me! I had already taken two years of psychology classes for my major in grief counseling, and I knew now that was headed in the wrong direction. But, during that course of study I had worked with several different professors and I knew they would help me make the transition to life coaching.

When I got home that day I called the school and signed up for the next session, and after that everything fell into place beautifully. Life coaching turned out to be the perfect fit for me. Life coaches use a combination of sociology and psychology mixed in with basic life skills to guide people to create the life they want, and during my studies I loved learning the many useful techniques and skills I would eventually use as a life coach.

In less than a year, I completed the course and earned my certificate; a few months later, I began helping people set personal and professional goals to chart their course for success. I was so thankful that my psychology professor had directed me toward the life I wanted to live, and after that I felt I should pay it forward by helping others find their own path to happiness.

It didn't happen overnight, though. Before I figured out my new path, I had been winding through a confusing series of transitions and changes, so getting to where I wanted to be was a step-by-step process. But I knew that Nicki wouldn't want me doing something just because I felt that it was expected of me, nor would she want me to pursue a path I wasn't comfortable with. My daughter would want me to be happy doing what I'm good at, and doing something that I enjoy. After returning to college, the vibrancy and dreams of the young energetic students on campus helped me to enter the world of the living again and to pursue my own happiness. Even though I didn't have control over everything in my life, nor did I have control over what could happen in the future, I knew that I could make some choices. And though I had chosen incorrectly in the beginning, I realized that perhaps God had put me on the grief counseling path for another purpose. God led me through twists and turns and eventually to a college professor who helped steer me in the right direction. The previous psychology classes that I took for a degree in grief counseling were used to help me determine what my personal goals were, and God had planted my professor of life span development as a catalyst to put me on the right path. Maybe by taking the *wrong* path I eventually found the *right* path, and then, once I was on the right path, I found my purpose.

During this time, I was still confused and grieving both Nicki and the loss of my marriage, and as it happened the life coach training program helped me tremendously. Life coaching is built on a system of listening to what people say, which was exactly what I needed at the time; my coach asked me questions designed to help me move forward rather than continue rehashing everything, and eventually I was able to think about what I wanted to achieve with my future rather than dwelling on the past. I learned that grieving is natural and takes years to fade, and often never completely goes away—but this is all right. I knew I was healthy, just sad and confused and scared.

At times coaching can feel therapeutic, but it isn't therapy. The basic tenet of life coaching is the belief that you hold the answers to all your personal questions and challenges in life—those answers are just hidden inside of you. A life coach's responsibility is to help you unlock the answers that are hidden inside, and unveil the key to success. With life coaching you're able to identify roadblocks that might be keeping you from moving forward. After you've identified them, you can remove the obstacles that are holding you back from your intended goal. With all the training I received, and with the help of my own life coach, I learned to look inside myself for answers. Sometimes when I had to go out into the world after Nicki died, now as a single woman, I felt like the world was spinning too fast for me: there were so many new technologies that had come out, and social media. To combat this feeling of chaos, my coach helped me to come up with new ways to adapt to all the changes in my own life, and I felt that I could suddenly see new opportunities to pursue my future, opportunities I hadn't had in the past. I wasn't sure what my life purpose was anymore, but I believed that I could rebuild my life.

I'll never forget my first coaching client, a twenty-eight-year-old woman who contacted me after she found my profile on the *Psychology Today* website. She was in a three-year relationship with a man but was no longer feeling satisfied, and worried the relationship was going to end if she didn't do something. But, she didn't know what to do to save it. When she first came to me they had been living together for a little over two years, but she had recently moved out because she felt they were going in opposite directions and had different goals: *her* goal was to marry him and start a family, but she wasn't sure *his* goal was the same. She liked to tell me stories about him, but I had to remind her that our sessions were about *her*. Not him. Although she was very successful in her job, she was uncertain that the hypothetical marriage would even work. I encouraged her to keep focused on herself, and she eventually came to realize that the basic problem was that she wasn't happy with herself. She discovered that she had relied on him to make her happy and that dependence was driving him away. As she learned to "create instead of *worrying about* creating," she began to finally experience peace in her life.

Another client of mine, a sixty-five-year-old man, had recently retired and subsequently didn't know what to do without his job. After six months of coaching, he realized that he still wanted to work—just not at the pace he had previously worked at. Through coaching, he charted a course and built his own consulting business which he now runs out of his home.

One of my most rewarding coaching success stories involved working with a divorced woman who didn't feel valuable after her husband moved out and filed for divorce. They had been married for twenty-years, and she didn't know what to do without him. To make things worse, she disliked her job. After a few months of coaching, she discovered that the stress she felt from working all those years at a job with very few rewards had led, in part, to the demise of her marriage. After eight months of coaching, she identified that what she wanted most of all was to go back to school and obtain her master's degree. So, she did!

The best decision that I made after my daughter died was to take the focus off my own hardships and focus on helping others to achieve their goals and dreams. For twenty-five years, I had lived the same lifestyle and then everything changed. I needed to find a new path in life, and find a healthy way to transition to this new future. It didn't happen overnight, but when it did happen it benefited me greatly. Helping people figure out their lives through listening and by asking questions is unbelievably rewarding, to say the least. Watching my clients chart a course to move forward in their lives feels *great*. Between life coaching and writing, my mind wasn't constantly consumed with sadness and thoughts of the past. I found a path, a purpose, and a balance that brought peace and harmony back to my life.

2007

*The great thing in the world is not so much
where we stand as in what direction
we are moving.*
—Oliver Wendell Holmes

The hardest adjustment I faced in the first two years after Nicki died and Jesse moved out was being alone in the house. I hadn't lived alone in decades, and that change always hit me hardest when I would return to the house at the end of the day and walk through the door with no one there to greet me. It was so quiet sometimes that I would leave music on just so that when I returned home there would be sound in the house. There were plenty of nights when I sat alone on the couch, books on my lap, thinking about the good old days when Nicki was healthy, and my marriage seemed secure. Other times, when I was cooking my dinner, I would see visions of Nicki jumping from her favorite chair, grabbing her camera, and running out the door into the back yard to photograph a large turtle that she spotted, or maybe one of the tropical birds walking around the edge of the lake. She had such an array of subjects: anhingas, herons, egrets, pelicans, and ospreys were just a few of the water birds she loved to photograph.

Being in the house alone without conversation brought continuous thoughts of Nicki running through my mind, and even though memories of her were comforting, they were also haunting after a while. Throughout Nicki's illness and for a while after she died, my family and friends came to visit, but in the end they had to resume their lives and I had to resume mine. But this proved hard to do; I felt an emptiness inside me, like there was a hole in my heart. Everyone was gone.

That feeling, the hollowness, was a huge wake-up call. It was apparent that I was having trouble adjusting to an empty house, so I sought guidance on how to deal with this from two wise men I highly respected. The first person was Father Ted from the Orthodox church where Nicki is buried. Father Ted was such a huge help to Jesse and our family during the three years Nicki battled brain cancer. He'd first been introduced to us when Jesse, during his senior year of high school, was given an assignment to compare four different religious denominations and write a comparison report. To do this he made appointments to interview a priest at the Catholic church, a pastor at the Presbyterian church, a minister at a nondenominational church, and Father Ted at St. Justin the Martyr Orthodox Church in Jacksonville. During his interview, Father Ted invited Jesse to attend one of the church's services to learn more about Orthodoxy. Jesse went to the church service the following Sunday and took Nicki and me with him. During the church service Father Ted prayed for Nicki and blessed her with holy oil; that afternoon, he came over to bless our house. It gave us comfort and peace to have a holy man of God pray for Nicki and our family, and even to bless our home.

When Nicki was hospitalized, Father Ted went to the hospital every day and blessed her with holy oil there. After she died, I visited her grave at the Orthodox church every day—I didn't know where else to go at the time. While there I often talked to Father Ted, and he helped me through the process of grieving. One bit of advice he gave to me then was that I should take my time to figure things out and not worry about moving too fast. He also told me not to sign any important documents, or to consider a serious relationship such as marriage for at least five years. At that point, getting married was the furthest thing from my mind. What I didn't know, though, was how important his advice was then, or that his advice would save me from making costly mistakes while I was grieving. I was thankful that I had a man of God to counsel me during that time. This was another example to me of God's work in my life: bringing Father Ted to us through Jesse three years before Nicki even got sick.

The other man I consulted was Dr. Rosenbaum, a clinical psychologist and the creator and director of the life coaching school where I took my training and earned my certification. He was such a smart man and quite optimistic, and I liked that quality about him. I had talked with him a couple of times before I began his life coaching program, but as we met more often Dr. Rosenbaum helped me to trust myself and to be aware of my feelings. He was a great listener, and having someone to talk to who let me figure things out for myself gave me peace. He always made me think before I made a decision, but he let me make it on my own. The first time I met with him he suggested that I read two books, *The Secret* and *Basic Freud*, which I did; both books ended up helping me tremendously.

Father Ted and Dr. Rosenbaum were not connected in any way, but they both impacted my life in significant ways. Right after Nicki died, when Father Ted advised me to wait five years before making any big decisions, that length of time seemed like an eternity. I listened to his advice and I trusted him because I knew that he had counseled many grieving people over the years through his church. I wasn't ever angry that God took Nicki: I just missed her companionship and love. I didn't want to feel sad anymore; I wanted to find a way to celebrate her life and work toward making myself better. And, with their help, both men encouraged me to take my time and trust in my journey.

Even though I won't ever completely stop grieving my child's death, I knew that one day I would be happy again. There are many people in life who have experienced even more loss than I have had, but grieving is not a competition. I'm glad I listened to Father Ted's advice, since I was not in a healthy state of mind right after Nicki died. I felt responsible for a lot of what happened, and experienced a significant amount of guilt over that sense of responsibility, but I later learned that guilt is common in grieving people, especially guilt associated with the loss of a child. As Nicki's mother, I felt that I was supposed to protect her and not let anything happen to her—especially not let her die. Talking to Father Ted and Dr. Rosembaum helped me look inside myself and forgive myself for the guilt that I was holding onto inside my heart.

Nicki's brain cancer caused a lot of changes in our lives that we couldn't control. Adjusting to being single after being married so long was an enormous change, one that, though it seemed like it happened overnight, really happened over a three-year period. My husband wanted a divorce and in the end, he never gave me a reason why. At the time when he filed for divorce I was shocked to find out that if one spouse files, the other will have to retain an attorney—the last thing I wanted to do while my daughter was dying. I would have been willing to go to counseling with him and it might have saved our marriage, but I will never know because he wouldn't go. I thought that if the two of us could talk openly about our marriage with someone it might have helped both of us, but he wanted out and made it clear that he didn't want to talk about our marriage. I guess that's why he left. Even though I begged him to keep trying for Nicki and Jesse, he wouldn't; he'd made his mind up and nothing I said or did could change his decision. Poor Nicki cried and pleaded with him to stay, but it was to no avail. It seemed selfish and cruel of him because it hurt her so badly, especially while she was fighting for her life. The timing couldn't have been worse for our family. Thinking back, perhaps it was best for everyone that he left, but I don't really think so, and now it's something we will never know.

Maybe I played a part in him leaving by neglecting him during the time Nicki was battling brain cancer. Maybe at the time I just didn't realize that was happening, but if I did neglect him it wasn't on purpose. Grieving does that to a person—it messes up your thinking. He had needs and I was his wife; I should have taken care of my husband, but I was so distraught from caring for Nick, helping when she was ill with vomiting and having severe headaches, seizures, and confusion. She needed my full assistance with almost everything; her driver's license had been taken away from her when she started having seizures and I had to drive her everywhere. There were so many trips to the hospital and so many times when I had to stay in the hospital for weeks at a time with her. I was the one who drove her to radiation treatments, two hours away from our house, during which we had to stay in hotels out of town so she could go to her early morning treatments.

I was mentally and physically exhausted from caring for her all day, and from worrying about her, and being up all night with her, and I didn't have the energy or the time to give myself to anyone else but her. Mike went to work every day so he wasn't responsible for her constant care. He was still living part-time in the normal world by getting out of the house and seeing healthy people, and this would have emphasized that, in comparison, our home wasn't normal. I'm sure during that time my husband felt alone and neglected. I'm sure he was lonely, as was I. But our daughter was dying. And instead of helping me he became distant and wouldn't talk to me about anything. He withdrew from all of us, refusing even to come to important medical appointments when the doctor requested that he be there.

I take the blame if there is any to be had, but I had to give one hundred percent of my time to my daughter. There was no one else to do it, and I wanted to take care of her. I'm her mother.

People say that time heals all wounds, and with time we all seemed to figure out how to move forward. The only difference was that we had to move forward with Nicki living in our hearts this time. Her absence will always be a huge void in my life, but I had to keep reminding myself that my daughter gave me an example of how to be strong. I watched her live as normally as possible while she battled cancer, and I aspired to be as strong and as brave as she was and do the same. If Nicki could finish high school and attend college with that brain tumor, then I could surely find a new path and resume my life. While in college she never told her professors that she had brain cancer because she didn't want extra favors. She was my hero and my teacher. She set an example of how to live under the worst of circumstances.

After she died, I worked hard to move beyond my feelings of self-blame. It was healthy for me to keep busy, and I found that the time I spent in college helped keep me from being in the house by myself all the time—which was probably a good thing, as I was reminded every time I walked into the house that my responsibilities to others were over. Raising my two kids, cleaning and cooking for four people: that part of my life was gone. Even though Nicki wasn't suffering anymore, my three-year term as her caretaker and nurse was over too. And even though I tried not to count the years that she'd been gone, I couldn't help it. I thought about how long it had been since I looked into her pretty blue eyes, and thought about how many years it was since she'd last given me a hug. How many years since the last time we walked on our beloved beach together. I thought about how I used to put pigtails—we called them piggy tails—in her hair. I would never be the mother of the bride, or hold her children in my arms. I was still missing a huge part of her life, but I felt happy when I could feel her spirit with me, and that was often. I accepted that God had allowed her to suffer and to die young, but it didn't stop me from counting every year of her absence, or from wondering why she'd been taken. The pain wasn't going away.

And so I decided that I would have to continue to live with a big hole in my heart. Her death is final: I can't see her, or touch her, or talk to her anymore. This is the reality of my daughter's untimely death. I will never hear her voice again, or get a hug from her again, and I will never hear her call out "Mommy!" from another room in our house. I miss the sound of her voice.

I don't know the exact moment that I felt I had accepted my daughter's suffering and her death. I had to for my own healing, and I had to do it for her, because she would want me to move on; I know that Nicki would be disappointed in me if I remained sullen. Even though not having her with me has been the hardest pain I have ever felt, I still had to make the choice to be happy so I could go forward and honor her life, and so I did.

REINVENTING THE BEACH HOUSE AND MY LIFE

2009

Staying in our beach house where I had raised Jesse and Nicki side by side as brother and sister offered me security at a time when I had lost so much. Being able to stay in the home where I had nursed my dying daughter was the best place for me to be; I didn't want any more change for a while. Everyone that had once lived with me in the house had moved on in some way or another, and I didn't want to let go of anything else in my life at that time. I needed something consistent, and I felt that the beach house was my only safety during the worst thing that could happen in a mother's life.

When I think about 2005 when Nicki died and Mike left, and I was given first right in the divorce to keep the house, I didn't realize then that keeping the house was a gift: that I could stay there. Remaining in the house was critical for me because it was filled with both memories and the spirit of my daughter, and I didn't want to lose any of her. It took me a long time to realize that Nicki's death wasn't just a horrible nightmare that I would wake up from; I kept thinking that she would come walking through the front door, yelling across the house, "I'm home, Mommy!"—and then she would give me a big hug like she always had. I knew that wasn't going to happen, but at least I could *imagine* that happening by staying. Staying gave me a chance to grieve her life, to heal in the place where it all happened, and to hold on to all my memories of her.

One of my fondest memories from the beach house is of the oak tree in our front yard. While Nicki was in high school, some of the boys from school would come over to our house on weekends to visit her, vying for her attention. One of the ways they tried to impress her was by attempting to climb the thirty-foot tree in our front yard—and that tree was a challenge! The boys' goal was to make it to the top without falling, and I can assure you that, had one of the boys succeeded in doing that, she would have been impressed! I can still see her shaking her head side to side and rolling her eyes as, one by one, the boys competed against each other for her approval and favor.

The tree has grown quite a bit taller since then and now tilts across the yard to the south. I've watched it gradually start to lean from my dining room window, blown sideways from years of the Atlantic Ocean breeze, tropical storms, Nor'easters, and hurricanes. Many of those storms happened after Nicki left us. Over time, I've wondered if the tree will eventually lean so far that it touches the ground, buffeted not only by a severe Nor'easter we had shortly after I was living in the beach house alone, but also by Hurricane Frances and Jeanne in 2004, and then in 2005, the year that Nicki died, tropical storm Bonnie.

But what worried me most, living alone in the house, was when the winds from the storms became so strong I thought for sure the leaning oak tree was going to fall across my driveway. It took a few years for me to get used to being by myself during storms, especially hurricanes. Thankfully, our beloved oak tree is very strong. But when I look at the tree from the window, as I often do, my emotions turn from fear into wistfulness, because the true beauty of our south-leaning tree is what it stands for, and the memories it holds.

The large oak tree still attracts my attention for its unique artistic beauty, in addition to fond memories of how hard it is to climb. But its true charm for me is the way the tree leans and bends: to me, it will always be a symbol of strength and perseverance, just like Nicki had been. I've often thought that God placed the oak tree in that very spot so many years before Nicki was born knowing that one day it would stand for everything we remember Nicki for: her beauty, her strength, and her perseverance. I get to be reminded of her when I walk through the house and look out the dining room window, or when I drive up to the house and pull into my driveway.

I could never leave the beach house, as moving would mean leaving behind the many reminders of Nicki in and around the house. And I had been apprehensive about changing anything for a long time because I thought that if I changed the house I would be losing my memories with Nicki. But when I saw my friends, living with their kids and husbands just as they always had, I began to feel that I should be free to live my life too. It was hard not to think or question God, *why me?* Why did my beloved daughter have to die so soon? I knew it was selfish, but at times, watching my friends with their families, I felt that way. Yet at the same time, watching how they were living their lives just as they always had helped me to gain strength so that I could not only live my life again, but *reinvent* it as well.

So, I realized that if I simply redesigned the house, my memories of Nicki would still be all around me and I would achieve some of the changes I needed. I've always loved decorating, but I never had the time or money to do much while I was raising the kids. But now that my responsibility to a husband and family were gone, it was a good time to beautify the house. And most importantly, I was ready to reinvent my life: it was time.

But before I started to decorate I wanted to preserve some of my tangible memories of Nicki. I had written for many years and throughout Nicki's illness and death continued to write; but, more than anything else, I was writing about Nicki, and what happened to her, and about our family that was no longer a family. I knew that I needed to pull myself together and honor Nicki like I said I would do by moving forward. At the beginning of 2010, I had started a new journal—but ended up writing sad poetry and laments about my life. So I looked online and found a pretty white leather journal that had *What If* written in gold letters on the front cover; I didn't want to use an old journal that I had lying around the house: I wanted to journal in something new and fresh, a journal I could use to write about rebirth and opportunity. I ordered that fine-looking journal on the spot, and when it arrived I opened it immediately and wrote "New Beginnings" on the first page.

Then I wrote a title for my first entry:

NO MORE FEELING SORRY FOR YOURSELF— EMBRACE THE NEW

I wrote a personal quote on the second page.

"If you allow your mind to dwell in sadness, you will never rekindle the beauty of new love."

This quote helped me to think more deeply about my life and about what I wanted for myself going forward. I wanted to fall in love, and to be in love; I wanted to share my love with someone again. I didn't want to get caught in sadness, unable to meet new people and experience new things. I knew that Nicki would not want me to be sad. She knew that I loved to write and I had continued my writing, and even made the decision to write a fiction book, a story of two souls who find each other by happenstance. I couldn't help but think, what if the tables were turned? What if it were me that died—how would I want Nicki to live if I were gone? I didn't have to search long for answers to that question: I knew that I wouldn't want my daughter to be sad or to stop doing the things she loved to do. Nor would I want her to stop growing or to stop progressing in her life. I would want her to find happiness. How would I feel if she went around moping all the time, avoiding her friends? Or worse—what if she gave up her dream to perform on Broadway? I would not want her to be afraid to face life like I had been doing. I wouldn't like that at all. It wouldn't honor me one bit. I would rather that my daughter honor my life with her enthusiasm, living her life to the fullest by acting and singing, doing the things she loved to do. I would want her to move to NYC and star in a Broadway show. I would want my passing to inspire her to pursue her passions, and to not let my death cause her to give up.

I had to calm my thoughts and focus on the here and now. Nicki wasn't here anymore and yet I was still focusing everything on her. I had to make my own choices and I knew that happiness is a choice. Jesse is alive: my son, who was always so helpful with Nicki. I knew that he wanted me to be happy, so I decided to focus on him and on my future. These thoughts helped me go forward and make healthy changes in my life that, I knew, would eventually bring me peace.

When I finished my diary entry at the bottom of the page I wrote:

Today I made the choice to become a strong woman. Now I will write about dreams of falling in love. I will experience a new birth, and create a beautiful life for myself and for others.

With that, I began to focus my energy on doing new and fun things. I got *motivated*. When my husband had moved out and purchased a property for himself using our money—and without my knowledge—I was granted the right to buy him out of his half of our house. When I did, it took an enormous amount of strength and a huge leap of faith, and I wasn't entirely happy to do it. But I put my trust in God and, as it turned out, putting my trust in God was the right thing to do.

It was a blessing for me to retain the house: it had been my home for fifteen years. Why was I being so negative? I had been given a gift. I wasn't ready yet to leave my house or my private beach, and now I didn't have to. I could continue to take my cherished daily walks along the ocean. While Nicki was battling cancer, she often walked along the ocean by herself to clear her mind and to relax. I'm sure she did a lot of praying too. The ocean waves help me to relax too, as they must have done for Nicki. There is something about the sound of the waves softly landing on the shore that pacifies me. When I look out over the water, I gain reassurance and strength, and I feel free and alive.

I wanted to stay right where I was in the beach house so that I could make ongoing memories on that same beach. I loved my house and cherished the memories that my family had made in it together; I had raised Jesse and Nicki there. But that was over, and everything had changed. I wasn't honoring Nicki, or really anyone, and especially not myself, by moping and feeling sorry for myself. So instead of moping around in the house, I decided I was going to spruce it up. Now that I was going to remain in the house, I could do anything I wanted to make it a reflection of my new life. And it was time to step into the new.

So with Nicki's strength in mind, I took my first step into the unknown. I put one foot in front of the other and started walking again with the living. I learned that when something bad happens unexpectedly, it can steer you off course whether you like it or not. And when things spiral out of control it seems impossible to stop the descent. Nicki's brain tumor had been like that. Life gave no sympathy to her disease, and during the time that Nicki was sick it seemed like God had deserted us. But He had not—He never does that. Watching Nicki's mental strength and her fierce fight even when she hardly had the physical or mental strength to continue reminded me that if she could do it, then so could I.

I found comfort in this Bible verse:

"Do not be anxious about anything, but in everything by prayer and supplication with thanksgiving let your requests be made known to God. And the peace of God, which surpasses all understanding, will guard your heart and your mind in Christ." (Philippians 4:6-7)

I believed that remodeling the house would be a great project for me, and it would help me mentally to bring new and fresh things into my life. It would keep me busy at night when I felt most alone, and would help keep my mind off missing Nicki. It might even open new doors of opportunity. The house hadn't been updated since we bought it new in 1991 and, looking around, I could imagine how refreshing it would be if I redesigned the house with a contemporary coastal look. I could also update the appliances and get rid of some of the worn furniture. I knew there was work to do and that I would need money for it, but luckily I could afford to have the work done because when I had bought Mike out of the house I refinanced and took some money. It would also be easy to work on the house since I was the only one living there. It could be a fun a project! The time was right to make changes and move forward.

So I sat down, gathered all my *House Beautiful* and *Coastal Living* magazines, looked through each page for ideas, and put a plan together. The next week I visited furniture showrooms and appliance stores, and looked online for more redesign ideas. I envisioned each room in the beach house with my coastal inspiration. The first thing I wanted to do was to get rid of the things that were worn to the point of not being able to restore: that meant taking the old carpet out and replacing it with hardwood floors. I never did like the carpet anyway! After the floors were replaced, I would have the house freshly painted, and then replace all the old counter tops.

Redesigning the house was turning out to be a lot of fun. I smiled when I thought about how much Nicki would love that I was doing this, as we had often had fun together changing her room around. I was venturing into new territory, and was still apprehensive that I might regret doing it—that I might be putting Nicki to rest forever by doing this. But I decided I would not let that worry stop me. I bowed my head in prayer, remembering a Bible passage from my Sunday school class when I was a little girl, one that had comforted me in past times of trouble. It's from the book of Hebrews, 13:5, NIV: "*I will never leave you, nor forsake you.*" I felt like the verse came from Nicki, and through it I felt her reassuring me that she would always be in my heart.

Even though I technically didn't need to change anything in Nicki's room, over time I forced myself to, because I knew that eventually I would have to, and it was better to try do it sooner than later. One day I walked into her room and couldn't smell her favorite perfume, Happy by Clinique. The smell had dissipated, and in that moment I realized that she had been gone longer than I wanted to be reminded of. Thankfully, fourteen years later, Clinique still sells Happy perfume, and I wear it quite often to remember her.

But the reality was that her room had become void of her smell, her warmth, her laughter—they were no longer there. She had left the room. I don't remember exactly when it first started, but when I went into her room I would feel a huge dark wave of grief come over me, and I couldn't stop it. The wave came so often that I became familiar with it, learned to ride it until it went away.

One day, cleaning out her closet, I found her photo albums. I pulled them down from the shelf one by one, sat on her bed with the albums spread out across her bedspread, and began looking at the photographs one by one. The first book was from 2003. I carefully, slowly turned each page to take each photograph in, one at a time. I was reminded of how much Nicki loved capturing images with her camera, a Christmas gift from her paternal grandparents. She loved it so much that she carried it everywhere with her, taking spontaneous snapshots:

moments in time. We didn't know that Christmas of 2004 would be her last Christmas with us.

It made me wonder if her habit of taking her camera with her everywhere, photographing her favorite things in life, was so that she could leave us photographic memories of times spent with her. When I opened the second album I saw a photo of our private path to the beach. She had photographed the path many times but this picture was different from the others: it told a story of our relationship as mother and daughter. I had walked in front of her on the path that day, and she stayed behind me with her camera snapping pictures of every step I took. This photo was of my footsteps in the sand along the path.

Seeing the picture of my footprints before me made me think about our many walks together on the beach and our many conversations we'd had over the years. We talked about boys, school, her dad and I, and life in general. We had so many shared conversations, and the photographs all brought them back to me. We had collected hundreds of beach shells together--which I could now see sitting on her dresser in a large glass container, right next to a picture of her friend Ryan. I turned another page in the album and there was the picture of the oleander tree on Seawalk Drive. It was fresh in my mind. We were on one of our usual walks in our neighborhood on a foggy gray day when suddenly we stopped in mid-stride, eyes widening: the tree was covered with hundreds of tiny white flowers; on the ground beneath the tree was a blanket of hundreds more white petals. Of course, Nicki had her camera with her and snapped it all, *click-click-click*: the street, the sky, and the tree.

That was our Nicki: she had a way of taking hold of

every moment and capturing it with her camera. As I sat with the albums I took a deep breath in, then exhaled, and thanked Nicki for taking me down memory lane in such a creative way. There were many more pictures in her album, but now I closed the cover and held it close to my heart. I didn't want to look at any more pictures. I missed her so much: I missed the walks we took together, and I missed watching her with her camera. I thought about the photo of the oleander tree. We must have walked by that tree a thousand or more times together over the years. I didn't remember the exact date she took the picture, nor did I know at the time that she would be leaving it for me as a reminder of so many special moments together as mother and daughter. I had never seen the oleander look as beautiful or mysterious than the day she photographed it with me.

I still walk by the oleander tree and always feel her spirit, but I am also reminded that the lovely white flowers from the oleander are poisonous, and can be fatal—just like the cancer that was hiding in Nicki's head. Perhaps her photo of the oleander is to remember that something deadly can hide inside of something beautiful.

When I was finished looking through her photos, I put each album back on the shelf one by one and walked out of her room. I was struggling with the natural order of life: parents are supposed to die before their kids; burying my teenage daughter felt wrong. Everything that belonged to her also had memories attached, and that's why I hadn't been able to change a thing since she last slept in her room. I was holding dear to the memory of the last time I kissed her and said goodnight to her as she slept in her bed.

Over the course of twenty-three years, I had twenty-three journals full of feelings, emotions, and anything and everything about my kids growing up. I also stuffed my journals with cards and photographs. I had CDs and DVDs full of the kids' recitals, their sports activities, and events from every school year starting with kindergarten and continuing all the way through high school. There were boxes of Legos, games, and all their trophies. I knew that sometime in the future I would be able to look at those again, but for now they were getting packed up and put in the closet. I sorted through everything individually, one by one, then boxed it all up put it away.

One thing that Nicki and I had had in common was a love of jewelry, and when I started going through her jewelry box it was extremely emotional for me. She was so neat and orderly and had organized every piece perfectly in its place in her jewelry box. Every piece was personal and held some sentimental value. Most of her jewelry had been given to her from family members or from friends over the years, with many pieces given to her while she was battling cancer. I could remember each piece of jewelry that she had and who gave it to her, and what it symbolized. She had bracelets, necklaces, and rings from family, classmates, and other close friends she'd grown up with, some with quotes or special sayings engraved on them. After she died, I gave some of the jewelry back to the friends who had given it to her, but I kept the ones with engraved quotes because they were personalized for her.

Nicki had saved all her acting scripts and monologues, even back to her first acting role as young Amy in a local theater production of *Annie Warbucks*. Looking through the scripts and the plays she had been cast in, I could almost hear her practicing her lines and reciting her monologues over and over again, preparing for the big performance. She loved acting and would practice and memorize her lines precisely. When I packed her scripts away I smiled and thanked her for reenacting so many Broadway shows for me over the years.

After compiling her scripts and monologues, I took down thirteen of her school yearbooks from where she had placed them one by one on a shelf in her room; opening them, I read all the endearments written on the inside covers. There were poems, stories, and drawings all written above signatures that had been lovingly signed with hearts, smiley faces, Xs and Os by classmates, friends, teachers, and advisors. Her school yearbooks were a reminder of how much Nicki was loved by everyone. When I was finished looking through each and every yearbook, I placed them back on her bookshelf. Next, I packed up her American Girl doll collection and her Barbie doll collection and put them in plastic bins for safekeeping. I found her wallet; inside were her school IDs and driver license, and folded up pieces of paper with numbers and notes written on them. I found several old cell phones that I kept because they had recorded messages still on them. How could I part with those? There were videos of her dance recitals, gymnastic competitions, swim meets, vocal concerts, musicals, plays, and other recorded memories from birthday parties, school trips, and vacations: all priceless memories of our little actress whose dream was to one day perform on Broadway. I closed my eyes and said to her: Nicki, your dream will come true, I promise. Your legacy will come to life on a Broadway stage in New York City. I will never stop sharing you and your dream. It won't be you on the stage, but your spirit will shine through the actress who looks like you. Your dream may not happen the way you dreamed it would, but it will play out for others on the stage the way God planned it.

I had always taught my kids to dream *big*, and to never give up on a dream.

When I was finished in her room, I rested my head on her pillow and gave a sigh of sad relief. Her memories were all neatly tucked away for safekeeping. And now, once I had stored all her belongings in a safe place in the house, I was ready to reinvent my home.

I planned to keep Jesse's room as an extra bedroom so if he came home to visit he would have a place to sleep. I had no ideas what I would use Nicki's room for, but I knew that in time I would figure it out. Getting started on the redesign was going to be a creative undertaking that I hoped would be fun and not too much work, and at this point I couldn't wait to get started. I had all my design magazines out and I could use the internet to look at coastal designs. First, I picked out a cool shade of mint and soft lavender for my accent color. I got rid of some of our old furniture right away to create space for new pieces, and I rummaged through all the pots and pans in the kitchen before cleaning out the linen closets sorting things into piles: keepers, throwaways, and the Goodwill pile. Once the unwanted furniture was gone, I had Italian travertine marble in a light beige tone put in throughout the house, everywhere except for the two back bedrooms that were Jesse's and Nicki's.

After the flooring was installed, I had the inside of the house painted with the Sherman Williams color

"Reflection," a soft gray that complemented the gray accent in the beige marble flooring. My kitchen is small, but I love the open-floor plan and its full view of the lake and Guana preserve—I like to look out the windows while cooking. I replaced all the appliances with brushed stainless steel, and then went to Mediterranean Designs—the local business where I had purchased the travertine flooring—and picked out marble counters for the kitchen. The kitchen cabinets were still in great condition, with just a little wear on the wood. I liked the aged effect and thought it added a rustic beach look to the kitchen, so I kept the solid maple cabinets and saved a lot of money by doing that, along with some of the original design of the house. My wine glass cabinet was refaced with beveled glass, then I had my electrician update the fluorescent lights with upgraded recessed lighting. But I couldn't stop there: I also had him install under-the-cabinet lighting. Finally, my kitchen design was complete: it had fresh paint and was full of fabulous marble, updated lighting, and stainless steel appliances.

Things were moving quickly; I was making progress and ready to add new coastal furniture. I wanted some distressed pieces, so I went to antique galleries and furniture boutiques around the beach, where I found and purchased two beige recliners with rattan arms and a white leather sofa for the living room. My dining room table and chairs had been with me since 1981, when my husband and I purchased the set from a young couple in Atlanta after we moved there from Michigan; the kids were four and three at the time. The dining set had belonged to the couple's grandparents, and by now it must be around one hundred years old. The set originally had a yellow pickled lacquer finish, a look that was popular during that era. It wasn't popular with me anymore, though, so I stripped all the lacquer off the furniture, painted it with chalk paint, then softly sanded the edges for a distressed look. That antique dining set is still one of my favorite furniture pieces: it has two extensions, four chairs, and two arm chairs. Along with the dining room set, I kept some other favorite furniture pieces for sentimental reasons, but the last piece of furniture I bought was a white solid wood distressed buffet table, a gem from Cottage by the Sea in Jacksonville Beach. Above the buffet table I hung a large framed picture of the Atlantic Ocean—and then my formal sitting room was a coastal dream.

After that, I installed hardwood floors in Nicki's room. I knew she would like that and I wished I had done it while she was alive: she would have liked to design her own room. I had to take everything out of her room to have the floors installed, so I made the decision to get rid of her mattress. Jesse took her headboard to his apartment. Once the floors were installed, I decided that I didn't want to make her room a bedroom. The two back bedrooms that my kids had slept in while growing up were not serving the same purpose anymore, and I only needed one extra bedroom in the house. It made sense that I would keep Jesse's room so that when he came home to visit I would have a bed for him to sleep in, though he only came home for rare visits and occasionally for holidays. He took his bedroom furniture when he moved out after high school, so now it became a guest room with a bed, two small nightstands, a bench, a desk, and a chair. I had the walls painted a soft Mei Mei green, and thought that anyone would be comfortable sleeping in his room: it looked polished and refreshed with the new dark wood floors.

While Nicki's room would be used for something other than a bedroom, I could not leave her room empty. I don't like empty bedrooms—they feel cold and sad. *Trust your heart*, I said to myself. I prayed and thought long and hard on how to best honor her, putting a lot of thought into how to redesign her room. I missed her every day, but knew she would be cheering me on with whatever I decided to do. Nicki always wanted me to be happy and healthy.

A year after Nicki died, I had called her pediatric oncologist at Nemours Children's Clinic, Dr. Pitel, to speak with him about creating a foundation in Nicki's name to help other young adults with cancer. He agreed that it would be a wonderful way to honor her and help others like her, so in 2006 the Nicki Leach Foundation, a 501(c)(3) nonprofit organization, was born. The foundation gives modest grants to young adults with cancer so that they can peruse their educational dreams and goals just as Nicki wanted to when she battled cancer. The foundation also supports funding for glioblastoma research in young adult tumors.

When I redesigned my house, the foundation didn't have an official office to work out of, so Nicki's room became the Nicki Leach Foundation office. After setting up Nicki's old room as a new office, the beach house redesign was complete: gorgeous marble floors, marble countertops in the kitchen, updated lighting, fresh painted walls, and new coastal furniture. My house was nineteen years old, but it suddenly felt brand new. It was hard at times, but doing it was fun, and when I finished the work some of my neighbors came over to see what I had done. That made me happy because I had been hiding out inside for a long time. I was surprised when they asked me if I would give them some ideas on how to redesign their own houses, and I happily did. Later, one of my neighbors gave me a large marble coffee table for helping her with her house, which I put in front of my new white couch. She also gave me a large Chinese painting of a very old tree with a red bird sitting on a branch—that, I hung above the buffet table. Being kind to one another is always a blessing.

MY SANCTUARY

2011

One morning I woke and lay in my bed thinking, had it really been two years since I redesigned the house? Yes, it had—and I suddenly wondered why I hadn't changed my master bedroom when I did the redesign. I guess I was comfortable enough with the way it had always been so I'd left it alone. But I wasn't comfortable with it anymore. For twenty-one years I had slept and prayed in that room— maybe a million prayers!—but since recently it had just been me sleeping alone I hadn't thought much about changing it. Nobody came in my bedroom but me, and I'd never thought of my bedroom as romantic—especially not my bed. It had been six years since a man slept in my bed with me, and that man was my husband. As I lay there thinking, I longed for a man's strong arms to hold me. The sun was shining through the slats in the blinds, and as I watched the sunlight beams dance across the ceiling I thought I could feel him in my soul. *Who are you?*

I had kept myself busy for two years redesigning the house; I had created a foundation in Nicki's memory; I had accomplished all the things I wanted to do. I had reinvented my life, but I was alone. Why am I alone, I thought, am I not desirable? Of course I'm desirable—he finds me desirable—but who is he? I missed having a man in my life. I wanted to roll over and feel a warm body beside me. I wanted to feel a pair of strong arms around me; I wanted a man to protect me. I wanted companionship and love, a man who I could share my life with.

I rolled over on my side and thought, *why am I still sleeping on the mattress that my former husband and I slept on together?* At the very least I could get a new mattress. That thought was enough for me to go out and buy myself a new one. But I didn't stop there: I bought a white four-poster bed frame, satin sheets, a gorgeous bedspread with gold and white sea shells, and a blue cashmere throw.

When the bed was delivered, I put on the satin sheets, the blankets, and the pillows, then I put the throw at the bottom of the bed. It was incredibly pretty, and I was so happy with the way my bed looked that I kept going and completely redesigned the rest of my bedroom! I bought a three-foot dieffenbachia plant and a marble pot, and put it by the bay window in my sitting area that overlooks the lake. Then I placed my white velveteen loveseat at an angle in front of the window, and positioned my rattan glass-top table in front of the love seat. I put a floor lamp beside the couch for reading, and a white shag rug at the foot of my bed.

My bedroom was transformed into a romantic palace. No longer was it just a place to sleep, but a peaceful place where I could wrap myself up in my cashmere throw with a morning cup of Sumatra and watch the sunrise over the lake from my bay window in the sitting area. The next day, I went out and bought candles and put them all around the room, and that evening lit the candles, poured myself a glass of wine, put on a new lingerie sleepwear dress, and stared at the reflection of the moon on the lake outside my window. When I got in bed, I pulled my new satin sheets over my body and turned the lights off. I rested my head on my satin pillow and closed my eyes. I lay there relaxing under the covers, rubbing my legs across the silk sheets. I thought about him. *Where are you?* I whispered out loud, and then fell asleep.

Good morning, spring! We were experiencing the most comfortable weather in north Florida. I think spring is the best time of year to do almost anything outside, especially yard work. Since I had nothing more to do on the inside of the house, and I was pleased with the results of my hard work, I wanted to tackle the outside next. It made me feel good when friends came over to visit and commented on how they liked that I had made the house a reflection of my new life. Those comments from friends and family made me feel good, and reminded me that I should spruce up the front yard so when they came to visit and walked up the long slate sidewalk to my front door they would feel welcome.

I often flashed back to twenty years earlier: the day my realtor drove us to the house and I fell in love with the outside even before seeing the inside. And when I'd walked inside, and seen the view of the lake in the back yard, it felt like home. I was thankful that mother nature had designed the back yard of the house so beautifully that I didn't have to do a thing. The view still takes my breath away; I spend a lot of time sitting in my yellow Adirondack chair on the deck, writing, enjoying the sound of the waves and the chirping birds, and the moist air from the ocean breeze on my skin.

Deciding to begin renovating the exterior of the house, I bought colorful flowers to plant in my flower boxes, a new white mailbox, and house numbers that matched the outdoor light fixtures, before hiring a painter to redo the door, window boxes, and shutters. When all of that was finished, it was time to tackle the yard work. Trimming the oak tree was going to be an important part of creating curb appeal, so I called a local tree-trimming company to trim Nicki's favorite tree. When the trimmers arrived and began their work, I watched from my dining room window as they cut small sections of branches to balance the limbs. I thought about Nicki and talked to her in my mind, letting her know that I was taking care of her tree. After all the trees in the yard were trimmed, my lawn service came to cut and fertilize the grass, and to trim the shrubs that lined the front of the house.

The next day I had the house power-washed. I'm always a little nervous about power-washing the house because the outside is made of coquina. Coquina comes from the Spanish word for "cockle" and "shellfish": it's a sedimentary rock composed mostly of the mineral calcite. Contractors and builders use it to create texture and to add a coastal or beachy look to the exterior of houses like mine—another one of the elements of my house that I liked.

Coquina is mostly used in Florida; it was often used in the oldest city, St. Augustine, which is only ten miles south of where my house is. Builders have been using it for over 400 years: they used it for building forts, as coquina is soft so that enemy cannonballs would sink into it rather than shatter or puncture the walls. This was the reason builders started using it on the exterior of houses. The old fort in St. Augustine was one of Jesse' and Nicki's favorite places to go: Jesse liked to walk the grounds of the old fort, and Nicki loved the homemade fudge and candy in St. Augustine. We used to go to St. Augustine as a family every Fourth of July to watch the fireworks from the Bridge of Lions. When

Jesse got his driver's license, he and Nicki would go there together. On July 4, 2004, Jesse took his sister to see the fireworks for the last time. It had always been her favorite holiday.

Because of this special material, the workers use a gentle cleaner instead of a harsh chemical, and when they were finished, the beach house at on Coastal Oak Circle was sparkling clean. The best part of all was picking out and filling the boxes with colorful flowers: yellow daisies, yellow coreopsis, dahlias in lavender (expressing dignity and elegance), and marigolds in orange, red gold, and mahogany. The finishing touch was having all the mulch removed and replaced with white stone. The stone looked so good that I continued it along each side of the long sandstone sidewalk that leads to my front door.

The day that the outside work was complete, I walked to the end of my sidewalk and turned around to face the front of my house. I stood there and wondered if my house would ever completely feel like a home again with only me living in it. But I couldn't go back, even if I wanted to. I had changed so much of what the house had been. I took a deep breath, then released the air with a huge sigh, releasing all the stress and worry. Standing there in front of the house, I thought about the past six years. I had changed my house so much from the way it was when everyone left home. Indeed, everything in my life had changed even if I didn't like it, especially during the time leading up to Nicki's death. All the changes began when she was diagnosed with cancer, and then life changed again when she died—and again when I got divorced, and again when my son went off to live his own life. Although kids grow up and leave home to pursue their own dreams and to live their own lives, burying your child is not normal. These thoughts were still in my head, and I'm not sure they will ever completely go away.

I couldn't take my eyes off my front door. My emotions were stirring and my heart was heavy. I had kept myself busy for six years, changing almost everything in my life so that I could move forward. I thanked God for the many friends who stood beside me and supported me through it all. I felt strongly that changing the look and feel of the house was the right thing to do, and that I had taken care of what I could so that I would be able to move beyond the past and into the future. I was too young to be alone; I wanted a man to share my life with, and I knew that I had to let go of some of the past to find love again.

I will hold every memory of those who lived in the house with me in my heart forever. I thought about my marriage, and how happy Mike and I were when I gave birth to our first child, a healthy boy with a name chosen from the Bible: Jesse, the father of David. Then I thought back to when I gave birth to our healthy baby girl. We named her Nicolette, as I just liked the name, but called her Nicki because she was petite and she had a bubbly personality. I had no way of knowing that she would only be with us nineteen years. I was thankful that God gave us that time together in the ER before she went into a coma when I told her to go into the arms of Jesus. That's when she dropped my hand and I told her that "Mommy will be all right."

She would be happy now, because I *am* all right. My daughter, Nicolette Beverly Leach—Beverly after my mother. Just saying my daughter's name out loud made me sad. The void I carry with me will stay with me forever, only one day filled when I am united with her again. I took another deep breath, and wondered if I was strong enough to completely walk away from the past, knowing that it would always be a part of me even as I went forward. I knew that my past included everything, all the way up to me standing at the end of my sidewalk staring at my front door.

I took another deep breath and exhaled. Then I put one foot in front of the other and began to walk forward. One step, two steps, three steps...walking until I was standing on my porch right in front of the door. I put my right hand on the handle, opened the door, and stepped inside. My eyes went through the house, through the redesign, and passed over all the changes that I had made to the house. My eyes fixed on the view in the back yard, just as I did in 1991 when I first walked into the house. I saw the view of the lake where the ducks swim and the white birds wander around the bank to catch fish. It was the beauty of the lake and the allure of the wildlife. It was the Guana preserve, and the surrounding nature preserve, that took my breath away in 1991, and did once again as I stood there.

I closed the door behind me, and with that I closed the door on much of my past.

I had transformed our beach house into a beach retreat.

I heard Nicki's voice: "Don't frown because it's over—smile because it happened."

Just as I had suffered and grieved in the house, I would also heal here.

The mere fact that I stayed in our family home after my husband moved out and filed for divorce, even as our beloved daughter was dying, was a testament to my strength, a strength I didn't know I had then. Two years had passed before I gave myself permission to move on. But now it was time: time for me to let go of the past.

Time is something we cannot stop, but we can move and heal with time. The past is the past. I've resolved many hurts from my past and made a choice to be happy. Change is inevitable and healthy. No one can know ahead of time what tomorrow will bring because we are not in control of tomorrow, but we can at least dream and manifest love.

GOD IS AT WORK ON OUR BEHALF—
EVEN IF WE DON'T KNOW IT
AT THE TIME

Little did I know that during the two years I spent redesigning my house, I was also building a career.

While I was redesigning the beach house, my neighbors had been watching; they were curious about the renovation, and a few later asked me if they could come over to see what I had done to the house. I hadn't seen many of my neighbors since Nicki died, so I decided to have a neighborhood open house and invite everyone. I picked a late Saturday afternoon to invite everyone over for a wine-and-cheese get-together. I was eager for their opinions, and happily surprised when almost everyone showed up. It was fun seeing my neighbors, because I hardly ever got to see the people who lived on the other side of the circle. I should have known they would be curious: it's a known fact that news travels fast in small communities! It was a good idea to invite everyone over because I hadn't been very social with many of them in a long time, and I thought it would be a good way to thank them for helping our family when Nicki was sick. Those who came were very kind, and they must have liked the way I designed my house, because later a few of my neighbors asked me for advice on how they could redesign their own houses.

A few weeks after having my neighbors over, word spread outside the neighborhood and into the surrounding beach community that I had redesigned my house, and soon a few people contacted me. They wondered if I would be willing to look at their houses and give them ideas on furniture choice and placement of their existing furniture. And then one day Priscilla—a realtor friend of mine—called and asked if she could stop over to look at my house. Shortly after Nicki died, Priscilla had obtained her relator license and moved to Miami for a couple of years to work with a large home-building company. I was happy that now she was back in Jacksonville, and excited that she was coming over, since she was selling a lot of new homes that had been professionally staged and I very much valued her opinion. Priscilla knew that I had a talent for making rooms look pretty because I had helped some of our mutual friends with their houses in the past. She wanted to catch up, so I invited her over for coffee. She had been to my house many times in the past, but it didn't look anything like it did the last time she was over, and I figured that she would be surprised when she saw how I changed the house from the original design.

She came over on a Saturday afternoon. I watched from the dining room window as she pulled into my driveway, got out of the car, and walked to my front door. Her eyes were busy taking everything in: the white stone that lined my sidewalk; the new shutters; the flower boxes filled with petunias, marigolds, and verbenas; and the simple shelled wreath I had placed on my freshly painted door. To add a special touch, I had found a turtle doorbell ringer.

I met her at the door and we immediately hugged as she scanned the room with surprise.

"Oh Bunny, this looks fabulous," she said, smiling.

I walked her around the house and showed her all the rooms. She thought everything looked fantastic, which, coming from a realtor who saw so many houses, made me feel great. She especially liked how I created so much open space simply by rearranging the furniture to fit the room properly. There are secrets to making a house look bigger through furniture arrangement and by installing proper lighting, and I made sure to do all these things in my small house. Priscilla also commented on how much she liked my furniture choice following the coastal theme.

After I walked her through the house, we sat down in my kitchen overlooking the lake, and talked while enjoying coffee and pastries. It had been a long while since I had afternoon coffee with a friend, and it sure felt good. Priscilla told me about her time selling houses in Miami and shared with me how much her business had grown. The reason she came back to Jacksonville was to sell homes in Nocatee. Nocatee has been under development for years and is the third best-selling community in the nation, so Priscilla had come back to sell houses there.

When she told me that she could use my help staging her listings, I smiled from ear to ear. I was surprised when she told me that most homeowners don't know how to prepare their houses by getting some help and advice from a stager before having it listed to sell. She also told me that all houses need some staging before they can be listed for the seller to get top dollar. Then she asked me if I would help her by staging some of her listings. I immediately said yes. I hadn't thought of getting paid for staging and redesigning other people's houses. I never had the time to do it while the kids were in school, and though Nicki and I had changed some of the rooms in our house to make them look better over the years, redesigning her bedroom several times and painting an accent wall, that was about it. I've always been fascinated with decorating and have subscriptions to *Coastal Living* magazine and several *House Beautiful* tabletop books, but I had never formally redesigned other people's houses, so I was thrilled when Pricilla wanted me to help her.

After meeting with Priscilla, I first enrolled in a local school and completed the program to obtain my home staging and redesign certification, and then became a member of RESA, the Real Estate Staging Association. Then, I began working with Priscilla as her stager, eventually working for other realtors in the area.

Of course, one thing leads to another, and after I began staging and redesigning other people's homes I found that it fit in with my life mission: helping people transition. Just as life coaching helps people to find their purpose and to create the life they desire, helping people stage their homes helps them move forward in their lives. Home staging is extremely rewarding for me because I enjoy helping families and individuals transition the way I had to. Moving is chaotic and stressful, and when I stage an individual's or family's house I want to ease the worry and stress that moving can cause.

Through my staging and redesign training, I developed a process that I use when I'm working with my clients. The first thing I do is walk through the inside of the house; after that I go outside and walk around. This is to get a feel for the homeowner's personality and what they like. I'm looking at the appearance and the condition of the house, as well as their furnishings. When I complete my walk-through, I sit down with the homeowners and go over the process. My goal is to connect with the homeowner and become likeminded so that we can achieve our best result. When homeowners and stagers come together in trust and commonality, the staging process is more relaxed and we get a better outcome.

The first step of the process is the hardest: removing things from the house. I had trouble with that part in my own house, but less is more when selling a house. Unnecessary stuff in a house creates clutter; and clutter is a home stager's worst nightmare—and a buyer's worst nightmare too.

Step two is when we put away all personal photos, or anything of a personal nature. It's important for buyers to envision the house belonging to *them*. We don't want potential buyers to be reminded that someone else lives or has lived in the house. It's a psychological reaction, but when buyers see the homeowner's personal photos it becomes a visual distraction. Buyers want to imagine that no one has ever lived in the house. We want the buyer to think of the house as theirs.

Step three is hands-on staging. The term hands-on is used because I use my hands a lot to move furniture and to place wall hangings and lamps and to move other things around the house. While staging, I try to use as much of the homeowner's existing furniture and reposition it in different areas of the house, taking furniture from one room and using it in another room. I like leaving enough space in rooms to enhance the beauty of the arrangement. If the homeowners' existing furniture doesn't work, then I find the appropriate size and style of furniture to fit. Then I add accent rugs, artwork, and mirrors to further beautify the rooms. Final touches such as pillows, throws, or table toppers complete the staging. The key is to keep things simple and bear in mind that less is more—especially when staging a house to sell. Ninety-nine percent of people first go online to view homes for sale before they drive to the house to walk through it. It's my job to make my clients' house look like a model home.

Although I love both home staging and redesign work, I find redesign to be more creative and fun. When redesigning a house there is less removal involved, and since the homeowner is not selling their house, they don't have to depersonalize it or keep it looking like a model home. In fact, redesign is *personalizing* a house by bringing in your favorite things, like I did to my house.

What I most enjoy about home staging and redesign is that I'm helping people transition through life, just like I had to. Staging homes is fun but there can also be challenges. One of the fun parts is that I get to pick out paint colors, and flooring, and find cool furniture and artwork. And, most importantly, I get to help my clients in a positive way so that they can move forward and transition smoothly.

Another reward from helping people transition through life is the friendships that I make and getting to know incredible people. I meet a wide variety of personalities, people from all walks of life and all different professions, which is always stimulating and rewarding. Newlyweds are fun to work with because they are excited to be embarking on a new life together. I also like working with couples who are starting families and want me to help them design their nurseries and baby proof their home.

I've worked with a lot of empty nesters, too, who usually call me to help them downsize when the kids have gone off to college or moved out of the house. This is when I get *really* creative, because some parents don't want to completely change their kids' rooms too soon after they leave home. That's how I felt about not wanting to change Nicki's room too soon. Working with homeowners who are moving because of a divorce is difficult sometimes, but I like to rise to the challenge and stay focused on the goal: do a good job so both people can move forward with their lives.

When I'm working with a homeowner who has lost a loved one, and that's the reason they are selling their house, I'm sensitive about how hard this is. I didn't want to move out of my house after Nicki died, but some people don't want to stay in their house after a loss. I feel deep emotion and sympathy in this situation. I'm careful with their feelings, but I also must get the job done for them in a timely matter. It's been proven that a staged property will sell faster and for more money than a house that hasn't been properly staged; additionally, staging saves homeowners thousands of dollars. The longer a house stays on the market the less money the homeowner will get for it, since when a house sits on the market too long, the homeowner will have to drop the asking price. I always try to be sensitive and to make sure that our time together is productive, so that the outcome is satisfying to their needs, and I feel honored and blessed that I can help people transition through these types of life situations.

I think I gravitated toward home staging because I've always been good at organizing, as was Nicki: we always had fun organizing together. Before she got sick, she once came to me and asked if we could start a mother-daughter organizing business. I wish we could have been able to put something together like that, but as it was, she was still in school at the moment, and then she got cancer and her time ran out. Perhaps, in the end, my new career in staging and redesign is her gift to me.

ESP: EXTRASENSORY PERCEPTION

March 2012

My master bedroom has always been my praying room and my crying room, but these days I don't cry as often as I used to. When Nicki was diagnosed with brain cancer, I was devastated and shocked because I had prayed for her from the time of her conception. Ironically, my prayers for her had been mainly for her health. Perhaps I had sensed something very early after she was born because I prayed more for her health than anything else—could I have felt something deep inside of me that caused me to pray primarily for that? I never thought one of my children would die before me, and I believe that God heard my prayers, but He doesn't always grant our wishes. I think God grants some of our wishes, but He doesn't do whatever we want just because we want it. My belief is that God follows His plan for our lives. He has a reason for everything, but it remains a mystery to me. I've put my trust in God and I try not to follow my own way, though it isn't always easy to do.

I'm not angry at God for taking Nicki: I know that wouldn't do any good. And I continue to pray for my son to be healthy, happy, and prosperous, because I do believe prayer is important. I pray for my own peace and comfort in life. I meditate, too, because it calms any anxiety and fear that I sometimes get. Meditating takes me to a safe place in my mind far away from worry, where I don't feel sad or lonely. I simply feel at ease and comfortable.

When Nicki began to exhibit physical and mental signs that something was wrong, and we didn't know what was causing her symptoms, I began a new journal and wrote my thoughts and feelings in it every day. Then when her symptoms progressed and became more serious, I sensed in my soul that she was going to suffer greatly. I didn't like that feeling at all, and hated to think that she would be in pain, but I couldn't get it out of my head or my heart.

It was around that same time that these premonitions progressed to ESP—extrasensory perception—known as the sixth sense, or second sight. I was no stranger to ESP either: I had experienced episodes of ESP many times in my life before; as a little girl around five years old I began experiencing strong perceptions and feelings that didn't come from anything that I could see, touch, or hear. The perceptions that I felt were deep in my mind, and mostly came on when something was going to happen, though I had no earthly idea *what* would happen. Thankfully, I was never afraid of these feelings.

My ESP reached its peak even before Nicki's behavior became odd and peculiar. I told her doctors that something was wrong, but they didn't take it seriously. They probably thought I was crazy or just overprotective. They were skeptical even though I told them that Nicki and I were strongly connected as mother and daughter, and her unexplained symptoms included trouble concentrating, headaches, and vomiting. I thought since I was her mother and had raised her for sixteen years, her doctors would have taken me seriously. But, they didn't.

ESP is especially powerful when two people are connected on the same level, as Nicki and I were. She was scared and so was I; we both knew something wasn't right.

It was almost as if I could climb in her body and feel what she was feeling. Even now I'm connected with her. There are times when I feel her with me and my skin tingles; I feel her breath like air on my bare skin and I get a chill. But the fear that was with me every day, for so long, while she had the brain tumor has subsided somewhat. I'm sure that time, prayer, and meditation helped ease that. It's as if fear and tragedy have given me both strength and caution in life, because I've had to accept that she died even if I don't want to. So, I choose to be happy because it's a better choice than living sad and depressed.

The years after she died came and went faster than I could keep up with. When I was living in my isolated world, engrossed mainly in prayer and recovering from my loss, I sought peace within myself and with God. Then, one day out of nowhere, I felt like I had awoken from a dream state: I realized suddenly that she'd been gone for seven years. How did seven years go by without me knowing? This awakening startled me, because I began to feel that something beautiful was going to happen though I didn't know *what*. I wasn't afraid; in fact, the seven-year mark was the point at which I had envisioned someone coming into my life. I had felt this person at times before and wondered if I was manifesting a new love.

It was in March of 2012, shortly after I finished writing my first book, *Turtle Shells: Heading Through Cancer,* when I felt someone's soul touch mine during one of my mediation sessions. My body became warm, and I relaxed into a dream state. I was connecting very deeply with someone; it felt like I was falling in love—but with who? I didn't know. Was he my soul mate? Had he found me? Yes: he'd come to awaken my senses. I immediately felt desirable, worthy—not just a sad, grieving woman all alone with no future. My soul mate was out in the world somewhere, but I didn't know where. My ESP was stronger than ever, and I was falling in love with a man. I had been manifesting love, and now, ready for love and romance, I longed to know who he was. I hoped that he would surface somewhere, someway, and someday *soon*. I felt that he was sent to me from God and that we would meet in time.

As it turned out, God created the perfect conditions for us to meet. My mystery man couldn't have known, nor could I have known, that our steps were being directed toward each other without our knowledge. We also didn't know that we would eventually end up in the same place at the same time, and when that happened our love would blossom. Only God could prearrange a meeting like the one he put together for the two of us! How could I have known, when our family made the move from Michigan to Ponte Vedra Beach twenty years earlier, that this would be where I would meet the man who was destined to be my future? God created something I thought only happened in romance novels, or in fairy tales.

GOD'S MYSTERY UNFOLDS

My life is coming together, I thought, as I woke to the sound of gentle waves on my beloved beach. I pulled the covers over my head and prayed to God in silence.

Dear God, I prayed, *I miss her, but I know you are holding my daughter in the palm of your hand. I know that she is safe. You promised me that I will see her again one day. Even though I don't know when that day will be, I'm holding your promise in my heart until that day arrives: the day when I stand before you. And then I will get to wrap my arms around my child again—I can't wait. Until then, my prayer is that you continue to grant me peace. Amen.*

I pushed the covers off and jumped out of bed. Then I went to my porch, opened the shutters, and looked at the sunlight through the trees. It's a gift from God to watch the sun rise over the Atlantic Ocean every morning. The rising sun is a reminder for me to "rise and shine," and never to give up on a dream, as well as a reminder to trust God, to be patient, and to await his timing.

As I watched the sunrise, I spoke to myself. *Always go forward, don't look back. Keep believing that your dreams will come true.* I thanked God that he created time, because time is a healer. I believed that one day I would experience beauty reborn out of ashes, as God had said that that he would take the ashes from death and out of them create beauty; I hoped the beauty would be a handsome, caring man. I wasn't sure if this was what God had in mind for me, but I hoped it was. I was ready to experience deep love with a man. I didn't know how long I had to wait, but patience and perseverance are just two of the virtues Nicki taught me, so I held on to hope. I couldn't help but think that Nicki was sending me someone because she didn't want me to be alone. She was, and always will be, my inspiration.

After she died, I'd had no idea what my future held or what I would do without her. True, fixing my house up had kept me busy for a couple of years, and I loved coaching and staging houses, but all the while I longed for my soul mate—and now I was ready. There was a reason I survived losing my teenage daughter. It happened, and God allowed it. I couldn't bring her back physically but I embraced her spirit every day. God had already blessed me in so many ways, and I felt my soul mate would come with time. The storm of losing my beloved daughter and enduring my divorce rearranged me, but it did not destroy me. The changes that took place in my life and the heartbreak I experienced when Nicki died had only made me stronger and wiser than I had ever been in my life. Just as my hero, Martin Luther King Jr., had a dream, I too had a dream: to go forward and create the life I desire to live. Like a turtle hatching from its shell, I went forward, breathing new life.

I thought about Tony, one of my staging clients who'd lost his wife to breast cancer. I had staged his house after his wife died because he didn't want to live in their marital house without her, living with all the memories of her. Part of staging a house is removing anything of a personal nature, and though this was hard for him, it also helped him to move forward and create a new life without her. The memories of her were just too painful to stay there, and he still had enough life in him to make new memories and hold onto the ones that he'd made with her.

People grieve in different ways: Tony wanted to move

out of their marital home as soon as he could after his wife died; I, on the other hand, wanted so desperately to stay in my house. After I staged Tony's house it sold within a month, as most staged homes do, and he packed up and moved to California. I hear that he's remarried now; they say that men move on faster than women. I don't know—I was searching for my soul mate, and I knew that when the two of us found each other we would share the rest of our lives together. We all need love and companionship to survive. No one wants to be alone.

MISSING PART OF THE PUZZLE

My bedroom has always been and remains my favorite place in the beach house for a number of reasons. I like the view of the lake in my sitting area, and I like my bed because it's comfortable and romantic. And maybe I also like it so much because my bedroom is the place where I have always prayed, so I feel close to God when I'm there. Before I get into bed at night I take a shower because the warm water relaxes me and I like being clean before I snuggle under my sheets. I always put body lotion all over me, usually "Seduction" body lotion by Victoria Secret. It was one of my ways to feel desirable. My husband and I shared a bed for twenty-four years, so it was a big adjustment when I began sleeping alone. It did help, when I was alone, that I felt my soul mate and I were deeply connected at night, though I still didn't know who he was. It had been a long time since I felt Nicki's breath on my skin; it made me wonder if her breath was being replaced with his breath. Our connection was so strong that I wasn't open to meeting or dating anyone else: I didn't want any distractions to get between us. He was in my heart and soul, and I knew that he wasn't far away.

During the day, I had more than enough staging and redesign clients to keep me busy, and the fulfillment I gained from coaching people to live life to the fullest and create the life they desired was rewarding. But all this didn't fill the romantic void in my life. Going into people's homes, seeing couples in love and living their lives together, just made me long for him more. Even though I was doing what I loved, I was always missing him—but who was I missing? Whose soul was touching my soul, and causing my emotions to stir? Most nights when I went to bed I tossed and turned with an overwhelming feeling that I was missing out on a great adventure. He was out there somewhere: I *knew* he was. Some nights I curled up in my blanket and hugged my pillow for hours. I'd forgotten what it felt like to snuggle up next to a warm body. Being in a relationship with a physical man seemed foreign to me. The few years that I had spent alone were very much needed, and gave me time to redesign my beach house and to figure out what I wanted to do career-wise. The right time for romance was now: this was the time for him to come to me.

Soon, my ESP came back stronger than ever and began working overtime. I felt like my soul mate and I would meet soon, but I wondered how, and when. He was still such a mystery, but I believed that it was just a matter of time before we would come into contact. I just needed to hold on and keep my trust in God, because our meeting was just around the corner.

SPIRIT MOVE

March 2012

Priscilla called me one day while she was out showing properties. She wanted to let me know that she had stopped by a new large condo development in Ponte Vedra Beach; she's always checking out new properties for her clients in the surrounding area, as Paradise condominium property is packed with charm and elegance. The Paradise community is nestled in a private part of the beach close to the Atlantic Ocean. Its property manager puts together social functions in the clubhouse for the tenants and those in the surrounding communities, monthly events that might include wine tastings, guest entertainers, and themed parties. Paradise clubhouse is beautifully designed and big enough to accommodate and entertain large groups of people, with a large kitchen, marble floors, and a large floor-to-ceiling marble fireplace. The area Priscilla was touring had been beautifully staged, too, and she was quite impressed.

But, best of all, she had some good news for me. While she was there, she had given the manager one of my staging cards and told her about my services, thinking perhaps that the manager could use my staging services to theme-stage some of the monthly events. As most things happen in life, one thing led to another, and Priscilla told her that I had had also written a book. This very much sparked the manager's interest.

"I've been looking for a local author to do a book signing here," she had told Priscilla. "We've never had one at Paradise, and we have a large book club. I'm sure the book club members would all attend. I would be thrilled to host a book signing for Bunny," she finished.

This was a surprise to Priscilla, as she thought they would instead be interested in my staging services.

"Oh, thank you," she said. "I'm sure Bunny would be honored to have you host a signing for her. She's lived at the beach for over twenty years, and her book reflects much of the beauty of living in the surrounding area. Why don't you give her a call? I'm sure she would be thrilled," Priscilla had said as she handed her my author card.

Priscilla went on to tell the manager about Nicki and the Nicki Leach Foundation. I couldn't help but think that God had set this up because the timing was perfect. My book had just been published, and I had two hundred crisp new copies of the book ready for my signing.

The property manager called me the next day and invited me to come to Paradise to meet her for coffee, and to see the clubhouse and set up the signing. So, the following week I drove to Paradise and met with her. She was a tall, thin, pretty blonde woman in her thirties, and was very well dressed. I gave her a copy of my book, *Turtle Shells: Heading through Cancer,* to read and then we set the date for my signing. I was very excited for the signing and to meet new people in the community who would be coming to support me and the Nicki Leach foundation. This was such a great opportunity for me to get publicity for my first book.

Priscilla and I arrived early to the event so that we could set up my signing table. When we opened the door to the clubhouse and walked in, we were both in awe. The clubhouse had been staged to look like a tropical paradise, and, looking at it as a stager, I thought it was spectacular. The entire clubhouse was decorated with a beach theme that included sand, shells, and turtle replicas that had been scattered around the room. I was surprised even more when I found out they had hired my son to DJ some of Nicki's favorite music. They had also hired a professional photographer to capture photos of the evening. Over one hundred people showed up for the signing to support me and to support Nicki's foundation as well. I felt honored and grateful—and I also felt that this was the start of a new beginning for me as an author.

Most of my time that evening was spent signing books and meeting new people. I signed over one hundred books, and then I took time to walk around and talk to friends and meet new people. I tried to take everything in: it was a magical evening. There was a buffet table covered with all sorts of mouthwatering foods, and when I saw that the large crystal centerpiece was filled with fortune cookies, a tear came to my eye. I had written a story about fortune cookies in the book: Nicki and I used to go to Chinese restaurants just to get a cookie for its fortune. We had a ritual: we had to wait to open our fortune cookie until after we finished our meals. Then I would make Nicki wait until I had opened my cookie and read my fortune before she could even open hers. It was a playful joke of ours, a fun thing we shared together. We always read our fortunes out loud to each other after we ate our food. Then we took our fortunes home and saved the tiny little pieces of paper in a special box. Our fortunes from over the years are now together in a pretty little box that I keep on my dresser. I miss doing this with her, and it remains one of my favorite memories of my daughter.

The event planner had supplied plenty of red wine and goldfish crackers for my signing—I'd also written about that in the book. The large glass buffet table was draped in white linen with so many varieties of beach shells meticulously placed around trays of sandwiches, bowls of potato salad, Caesar salad, and cheese platters. For dessert, we had white wine and cookies cut in the shape of sand dollars. There was more than enough food for all the guests, and we topped it off with chocolate Kisses. Lilies were laid on the tables beside long-stem wine glasses, each with its own turtle charm, the aroma from the lilies filling the room. The atmosphere was warm and inviting; it felt like we were at a fantasy beach resort—but then, we truly were.

My book signing turned out to be enchanting, so much more than I could have wished for. Everything about it had been lovingly thought out. The team put together many wonderful surprises for me, and when I saw that they had displayed Nicki's framed photography above the large marble fireplace, her images glowing from the firelight, I lost my composure. My heart was touched when I felt her spirit present. It was an honor to have my daughter's photography so exquisitely displayed. At the end of the evening, guest after guest came to me to tell me how they felt Nicki's presence touch them, and how her spirit was in the room that evening. It was a beautiful beginning for me both as a new author and as a mother who lost her child, at such a young age, to a horrible disease. As an author, I don't believe that I will ever experience a book signing that will top this one. It was a fairy tale evening, and even though she wasn't physically there, Nicki and I were both treated like princesses. And even though it was my event,

Nicki was really the one on display that evening, with the stage set to respect and honor her life and her memory. I had become an author because of her, and my first book signing will forever be an enchanted memory in my mind and heart. I felt loved.

And as love is a gift that keeps on giving, the very next day I was asked to be a guest on *First Coast Living,* a local television show that highlights national guests as well as people in the community. It was bittersweet to talk on television about my daughter and the tragedy that led to me publishing a book. But with this book I hope that I will bring awareness to a disease that is the number one cause of death in young children, and ultimately, I am humbled and thankful to have been given the opportunity to share her story with a wider audience.

SURPRISE

Spring is my favorite time of year. It was less than a month shy of the seven-year mark since Nicki died, and I missed her more than ever. I was writing my second book. My coaching practice continued to grow, and I was enjoying watching my clients develop and create the lives they had once only dreamed they could live. My home staging and redesign business was thriving, and I was happy that many of the people I met through staging their houses had become my friends—that thought made me smile. My work was rewarding and brought so many wonderful people into my life. God had blessed me with so many good friends, a loving family, and a great son who made me proud. I loved my work and the people I worked with.

So, what was missing?

I bowed my head and prayed.

God, I said, *you took Nicki home to be with you and you have blessed me in many ways. I know that I shouldn't be selfish, but I'm lonely. There is something missing in my life. Not something, but someone. It's my soul mate, God: I know he's out there because I feel him with me now more than ever. I know you sent him to me and that you will decide when and how we will meet—I just wish he would appear soon and fulfill the desire inside of me. Thank you, God.*

It was April of 2012 when I began to feel a change in the air. The beautiful spring weather enticed my college housemate, Terri, from my hometown in Ann Arbor,

Michigan, to leave the withering winter cold behind and come south to visit me. I was excited to see her and looked forward to her visit. During the time that we had roomed together in college we'd become like sisters; the last time I saw her was when she came to Florida and stayed with me for Nicki's funeral in 2005. That was seven years ago, and I missed her so much. My book had just been released, so the timing for Terri to come was perfect. It was a blessing that she was with me for the launch party at the Paradise community: it was heartwarming that she could be there for my first book signing, and that she got to meet all my special friends that night.

Terri was going to get me out of the house more to do some fun stuff, and I was so ready: I planned a lot of fun things for the two of us to do while she was here. Most of my time had been spent staging houses, coaching, and writing. In fact, I had been writing so much that I had a complete book: *Letting Nicki Go*. Spending time with Terri was huge at this point in my life. We had so much fun together, acting like college girls again. We took daily walks on the beach and ate at a different restaurant every night; Terri especially liked to go to restaurants that served fresh seafood. Almost every evening we were meeting new people and exploring new parts of Jacksonville, especially the beaches and St. Augustine. Being with Terri changed my mood from lonely to content. Having her living in the house with me helped to distract my mind from being completely obsessed with the quest for my soul mate. But it was an uplifting time, and I was still riding high from my book signing and my television appearance. Both Terri and I were ready to let our hair down and have fun!

It was a Friday night and I wanted to take Terri

somewhere special for dinner. Since we would be eating around sunset, I decided to take her to Fish Camp. I wanted to celebrate both Terri being with me and having Nicki's story published. I was ready to start a new chapter in my life. I felt that God was shining on me like the sun, and warming my heart, but I didn't know at the time that I was about to experience more than a new chapter in my life: I was about to experience a *rebirth*. Although Nicki continued to be ever-present in my mind and heart, it had been seven years since she died and I felt that I had finally reached peace with her death. Writing her story in *Letting Nicki Go* had been a healthy way for me to grieve Nicki, and to bring awareness to the reality of families with a loved one diagnosed with brain cancer. What I didn't know while I was writing the book, though, was that I had already met my soul mate and, in fact, mentioned him in the book—but only in passing. I had no idea at that time that our souls had touched.

And I had no idea that, when I chose to take Terri to Fish Camp for dinner, Nicki would come back in a big way— a way that I could have never imagined. The event that was going to take place at the restaurant would have the makings of a Broadway show. Little did I know that the script had been written, the stage was set, and even the actors had taken their places.

He spotted me from across the room and our eyes instantly locked. This was the moment I had been waiting for. This was what I had prayed for.

The curtain was about to open for act one.

WHEN TWO SOULS MEET

Fish Camp is one of the most popular restaurants in our beach community: the seafood is local and always fresh, and the restaurant has a spectacular view of the Intercostal Waterway. The only problem with the restaurant is that it's small and the seating is limited, especially for dinner, which can pose a problem if you haven't made reservations in advance. Since I wasn't sure of where I would be taking Terri until the last minute, I hadn't made reservations for the two of us that evening. So, when we arrived at the restaurant, there already was a crowd of people waiting for tables. I shimmied my way over to the hostess stand to put our names on the list for a table for two, but wasn't surprised to be told that there would be about an hour-long wait. That's a long time to wait for a table if you're hungry, but we were staying regardless of the time.

The weather was perfect, so we ordered a glass of wine and went outside to the deck to watch the boats on the water. The temperature was warm with just a little humidity in the air, and the sun cast a haze of orange and red over the Intracoastal Waterway. I sat in a yellow Adirondack chair; Terri chose a red one. We looked up at the evening sky above the water: there must have been a million shooting stars above us; they looked like sparklers on the Fourth of July illuminating the sunset. It was incredible! We didn't mind waiting for our table at all with a view like that, and the wait gave us more time to relax and enjoy the sunset and our friendship before dinner. We sipped our Rutherford Hill and reminisced about the past, talking about how we met. We were fifteen; it was at the

Jackson Armory in Jackson, Michigan. We were simple country teenagers with teenage boyfriends who were both drummers, but in different bands. We sat talking and giggling just like old times. The atmosphere was perfect: we were comfortable and not in any hurry to go anywhere. It just felt right.

We must have sat in those chairs out on the deck for at least thirty minutes when the aroma of fresh shrimp, oysters, and other mouth-watering smells coming from the kitchen enticed us to leave our deck retreat and go back inside to check on the status of our table. As soon as we walked into the restaurant, a friend of mine, sitting at the bar with her husband, spotted me, jumped off her bar stool, and came over to say hello. Her son Jamie had attended middle school with Nicki in Ponte Vedra Beach, but sadly Jamie had died five years after Nicki—in fact, from the same brain tumor. I knew her pain was still very raw since her son had only died two years ago. It seemed unusual that we, two grieving mothers, would be at Fish Camp at the exact same time. I thought, *there must be a reason that we are both here tonight.* I hadn't seen her in over a year; therefore, I was surprised to see her, and wondered what God was up to.

Grieving mothers seem to sniff each other out if they are close enough, and she had immediately found me out that night. When I saw her jump off her bar stool and come toward me, I recalled when her son was in the hospital during his final days. The flashback made me sad, and I didn't want to remember these sad times; I was moving beyond grief and hoping for a fresh start with someone that I could embrace the future with. But when I saw her, my mind went back to that time: we'd often met for lunch when Jamie was being treated at the Mayo Clinic for his brain tumor, and the Nicki Leach Foundation held a fundraising event at a local restaurant to raise money for the family. It wasn't that I didn't want to see her that evening, but there is always an underlying reminder of our shared loss and pain that comes back when grieving mothers run into each other unexpectedly. When we bump into each other we realize that we are not alone in our loss and pain, but on this particular night Terri and I were having fun and letting our hair down, and I didn't want to be reminded of death and dying. It seems selfish, but I was having so much fun, and everything finally felt free and easy. I just wanted the happiness to continue.

But what I didn't know was that this friend was being used to bring the past back but for a different reason than to make me sad: the reason she'd rushed over to talk to me was to direct my attention to a man standing across the room—the man with whom I locked eyes earlier. He was standing near the entrance, waiting for a table with an older man and a woman who looked to be about his age. He was handsome, a bit over six feet tall, with dark hair and dark eyes. We had been drawn to each other immediately; when I walked into the restaurant our eyes locked on each other, but a group of hungry patrons waiting for a table gathered in front of him and blocked us. Now Jamie's mom was directing my attention back to him.

"Bunny, do you see Dr. Jaeckle standing over there?" She gestured by nodding her head toward the handsome man that I was drawn to. "Didn't he take care of Nicki when she was sick?"

I hesitated for a minute before it hit me: that's him! I was so surprised. "Yes, he was one of her doctors," I said.

"Gosh, I hardly recognize him—it's been seven years now."

My mind flashed back to the day I took Nicki to the Mayo Clinic to be evaluated by a neuro-oncologist: Dr. Kurt Jaeckle. Nicki's pediatric oncologist at Nemours Children's clinic had sent us to the Mayo Clinic to see him. The oncologist had exhausted all his resources and didn't know what else to do for her. There wasn't a treatment that could stop her tumor from progressing, so he sent us to Dr. Jaeckle thinking there might be something he could do.

How could I ever forget that day when Nicki and I sat in the examining room, waiting on pins and needles, hoping that he could save her life. The memory was so clear to me. Dr. Jaeckle walked in wearing a white lab coat; I hadn't been with my husband for so long, and thought the doctor was handsome. Then he made eye contact with me, and I saw compassion in those brown eyes. I hadn't felt compassion in so long.

I'd looked away, though. My daughter was dying.

And now, it was him across the room.

"Yes, that's him. That's Dr. Jaeckle," she said. He had been her son's doctor too. "I'm going to go over to say hi to him. Why don't you come with me?" She took my hand and started pulling me toward him.

I dropped her hand and pulled away awkwardly. "I don't want to go over and say hi," I protested. "I don't want to revisit that time in my life. And besides, I've moved on from doctors and hospitals and clinics. You go."

It had been seven years since Nicki and I went to him, but I wasn't sure that I really wanted to revisit that time. First Dr. Jaeckle had evaluated Nicki's condition before deciding to put her on a clinical trial, but in the end it was too late for that: she died before she could be added to it.

Though it had been almost a decade, I didn't want to do anything that would put me back in that time, especially revisiting her final days. It had taken me so long to move forward. Grieving is a long process and I was just waking up and starting to live again, and hoping for new beginnings. If I went over to talk to her doctor, that might bring all the sadness back.

But, after she died I *did* go back and thank all her other doctors. I even took cards and poems to her neuro-surgeon, her radiologist, and her primary pediatric oncologist. But not him. Why? Why didn't I go back to see him, or to thank him?

My friend took my hand again.

"Oh, come on. Come with me!" she pleaded.

I shook my head. "No, really, I don't want to. You go ahead."

I wished her well, then turned and walked in the other direction. But something inside of me didn't feel right. Shouldn't I say thank you now that he's here right in front of me? Maybe that's why we were both here now, the reason we were all gathered together after seven years: so that I could say thank you. But, I thought, he didn't save her life: she died.

And yet, he was the man I locked eyes with earlier, and I felt something, a magnetic attraction. But I was going to do the right thing and let it go.

But wait! Could he be my soul mate? I was drawn to him even before I realized who he was.

That's when Deb walked away and I turned to look in his direction, watching her as she approached him. They faced each other and their mouths started moving. What were they saying? Why did I care? It was just a friendly exchange of hellos. So why was I being so resistant to go with her and say hello?

My mind kept telling me to walk over and join them. What was I afraid of? I started rationalizing everything from the past, trying to talk myself into it. He had taken care of my daughter; he touched her with his hands and even though they weren't healing hands, they were kind, gentle hands. I remember that much: he did what he could to try and save her life. Was I mad at him for failing? It wasn't his fault—we got to him too late. And besides, he couldn't have saved her anyway. He's not God. He seemed caring, but what if I walked over to him and he didn't remember me? What then? That would be awkward, and insulting, and disrespectful to Nicki. He would have to remember Nicki and me.

My mind was running wild, and I wondered what he must have been thinking with two grieving mothers, whose kids both died under his care. Now we were all gathered in the same restaurant. He probably didn't want to be bothered when he's out for dinner, just like I don't want to revisit that time by seeing him. And, I thought, he sees hundreds of patients every year and it was seven years ago. I didn't recognize him, so he wouldn't recognize me either. But we were attracted to each other when I walked in tonight and saw him standing by the door! We had been attracted to each other seven years ago, and we were still attracted to each other now. I *knew* he remembered Nicki: she was beautiful and special, and he must remember me too. I saw the way he looked at me.

That did it. I turned around to face him, then walked toward him. Memories that I didn't want to recall came rushing through my brain, taking me back to where I didn't want to go. I remembered the day Nicki and I sat in the examining room waiting for him, both of us scared and cold. It's always cold in hospitals and clinics. She was so sick and uncomfortable, and I was desperate, screaming in my head, *help her, help her*. I was a different woman then than I am now my mind wasn't my own: cancer was in control, not me. I figured that the doctor was probably used to seeing desperate patients, but we weren't used to being desperate or dependent on doctors. That tumor had changed our world from normal to chaotic overnight. Then my husband walked out, and we were all alone. We needed a man to help us, not a doctor. Doctors don't live in our world, and I didn't think he could understand how we felt or what we were going through.

But that's was all over now—it had been over for seven years. I was done with doctors. So why did I care about him? What was this night about, and why was he here? Why was I here revisiting this? Was something wrong with me? Why was I so afraid of the past and the truth? I shouldn't have been attracted to my daughter's doctor anyway, the first time we met, but I had been desperate and scared when my husband walked out and left me alone with her while she was dying. How could her father *do* that? But still, it was horrible: how could I have had such selfish feelings, especially then? That was just plain wrong! Plus, if I were to go over and talk to him now it would surely bring back even more sad memories of that time.

But he was the only one who had offered Nicki hope. I can never forget that. Indeed, I wrote it in my first book, that "her doctor at the Mayo Clinic gave us hope." He needed to know that, I thought. I must tell him. God could have worked through him to perform a miracle on Nicki, but He didn't because God wanted her, and so He took her. It wasn't the doctor's fault that she died. He wasn't Nicki's primary doctor anyway. Not one of her doctors had been able to stop the tumor from growing. He had been our last hope for a miracle.

It wasn't his fault. Why would I blame him? It was because I felt guilty. And now I knew the reason the three of us were gathered together. Without my friend, I might not have realized who he was, and maybe I would have let it all go. She was the catalyst between us. That's why she's here to direct me to him, I thought, and that's why he was there too. *God arranged this.* With those thoughts, my curiosity grew stronger, and my eyes stayed glued on the two of them as they talked. I tried to read their lips, and the magnetic powers between us became so strong that I found myself drawn to go over and join them. I was connecting with him.

I had already wiped most of the past out, especially anything that had to do with Nicki's clinical visits, doctors, and dreaded hospital stays. Maybe that's why I could barely put his name and face together when I first walked into Fish Camp and saw him standing here. I had left all the clinical visits in the past where they belonged. But we were in a different time now, and I had showed up here for a reason. And, I thought, he sure is handsome! I couldn't deny that I wanted to go to him, as I noticed that he kept looking over at me. And besides, I thought, it would only be a quick hello if I walked over.

About two weeks after Nicki died, I went back and visited all my daughter's doctors. I had needed to do that for closure: she had one oncologist, two radiologists, and a neurosurgeon. But Nicki and I were not as close to Dr.

Jaeckle as we were with the others, as he only saw Nicki five times, beginning long after her disease progressed. I don't remember much from those visits except that Nicki didn't like the nurse—she was cold and rude. So while I revisited all Nicki's other doctors, that was the reason I didn't go back to thank him or give him one of my books. But maybe the doctor and I weren't supposed to have closure like I wanted to have with her other doctors. Maybe something inside made me stay away from him, and now God was having us meet here at Fish Camp under different circumstances. Seven years after my daughter died was long enough to face him and begin life fresh. Maybe he was my new beginning. Was he my soul mate? This was a mysterious evening with the three of us together, along with Terri, my lifelong friend, all gathered in the same place at the same time.

Little did I know that something even stranger was about to happen... along with a plan, God also has a sense of humor.

UNEXPECTED FLASH FROM THE PAST

It was in 2006, one year after Nicki died, that Priscilla introduced me to a nice man who lives in our community. His wife had died from an undetermined cancer around the same time that Nicki did, and Priscilla thought that by introducing me to this man, we could provide each other companionship since we were both living alone and grieving our loved ones. Although he was an incredibly nice man and we had fun times together, the relationship never went beyond friendship and we both knew that it was never going to turn into marriage. I longed for my soul mate and it wasn't him, and as time passed we both knew that we should go our separate ways. We are all just looking for the right person. The separation was a hard adjustment for me because we had kept each other company during the critical time after our loss, and when we ended our friendship, I relapsed deeper into grieving. Once we went our separate ways, I didn't see him again or run into him even though he lived just two miles from my house. So naturally, I was surprised when Terri spotted him walking into Fish Camp that night. I was completely over the relationship, even though I still held deep respect for him, and that night was solely wrapped up in Nicki's doctor: nothing could steer my mind away from Dr. Jaeckle. I believe that everything happens for a reason, though, so for a minute I was a little curious why this other man from my past had also shown up that night.

Staring at Dr. Jaeckle from across the room, I remembered even more from our last visit with him in 2004. I pictured Nicki and I sitting in the examining room waiting for him to come in. When he walked through the door, he was wearing his long white coat. Pediatricians don't often wear white coats because they scare the kids, but Nicki was hardly a little kid—she was eighteen, and the only thing that scared her was that damn tumor in her brain. I observed her doctor cautiously as he performed tests on Nicki, and as I did so I felt his compassion and his confidence. I had liked that, and now, in Fish Camp, wondered if he would take the same loving care with me.

Whenever he examined my daughter, he asked her questions; during this particular visit, he asked her if she had been dropping things out of her right hand. She shook her head no and said that she hadn't. But later that evening when we were back at home she took a glass from our kitchen cupboard and filled it with water from the refrigerator just like she had always done—only this time, when she lifted the glass to her mouth, it fell out of her hand onto the floor and shattered into a million pieces, spilling water and ice all over the kitchen floor. The timing for this seemed odd, almost as if he had predicted it. But really, he had seen something on her MRI that told him this could happen: the tumor had progressed.

There were times when Nicki was stable, but soon enough she always had some bad reaction or side effect from the medications and the procedures. We went through all kinds of setbacks with our medical insurance, but finally our insurance covered her visits to Dr. Jaeckle, as he was the only neuro-oncologist in Florida. This is what delayed us from taking her to him earlier. Not that it would have mattered anyway: in the end, her disease had progressed too fast and, without a cure or treatment for her disease, it was just a matter of time before we would lose her. Dr. Jaeckle could only try to get her on a clinical trial as quickly as possible with the hope that it would shrink the tumor. But Nicki didn't have enough time. She was like an hourglass, and before the treatment got to her, she slipped into a coma. My soul mate told me later that the treatment, if used, still would not have saved her life.

Why was I afraid to say hello to him? Was I to avoid every sad memory from that time with my daughter? Could I simply embrace it and accept that there were clinic visits, medical procedures, and hospital stays that were painful for her to go through, and painful for me to watch? Although she suffered and it was difficult to watch her in so much pain, it was still part of our time together. I couldn't change the past, but I could accept what happened in the past and choose to go forward in happiness, trusting God.

I couldn't help but feel that there was a definite purpose that Dr. Jaeckle and I were meeting again under these different circumstances. How could I deny that? There was no mystery at all: it was fate, and was so apparent when I looked over in his direction and saw him standing there, staring across the room at me. He was magnetic, and I was being pulled to him. We were both feeling a power beyond our control, drawing us together, a force beyond our conscious minds. God has a reason for everything, even if we don't know it at the time. But this time I felt that I knew God's reason.

Then, Terri looked me straight in the eye. "Bunny," she said, "you have to go over and say hi to him. He was a part of Nicki's life. He saw her, he touched her with his hands. He tried to heal her. You gave the other doctors a copy of your book. Why not him?"

I had forgotten all about the book. I had to admit that Terri was making sense when she reminded me why I should go over and say hello, and I did want to go over to him—but I didn't know what to say. I wanted to know if he remembered Nicki and me. And he looked so handsome: I was very attracted to him.

The day we were at the Mayo clinic, and Dr. Jaeckle walked into the examining room, something inside me took notice, and it wasn't just his physical appearance. It was something else, but I had to let it go at the time. Here at Fish Camp, though, I wondered, *do I have to let it go* now? My daughter was sick then. I wasn't in a normal state of mind, so I had to deny any personal feelings; I hid them deep inside of me. But this surprise meeting was different. I felt desire, as though I were being pulled to him.

I knew that I had to walk over and say hello, so I did. And as I did so, I couldn't contain my big smile. I hoped he couldn't tell how nervous I was!

"Hi," I said, introducing myself. "Bunny Leach. Do you remember me?" Did I really think he wouldn't remember me?

"Of course, I remember you, Bunny," he said. He too had a big smile on his face. "In fact, we were just talking about you the other day." Oh, boy, I thought!

His brown eyes were amazing, and if it was true that he was "just talking about me the other day," then it seemed that God had indeed prearranged for us to meet. Our meeting was not a coincidence, no way. The evening was becoming even more mysterious. Dr. Jaeckle seemed a bit nervous too, like I was, but I could tell that he was very happy to see me. We were both acting a little silly. Plus, he was staring deep into my eyes, and from the big smile on his face I could tell he *definitely* remembered me.

As we spoke, he introduced me to his dad and sister, who were visiting from out of town, and although I was a stranger, his dad gave me a warm hug. I sensed that his dad was a compassionate man who loved his son dearly. I guessed this was where he had learned the care I'd noticed during Nicki's doctor appointments. It was also an interesting bonus that I got to meet his family while they were visiting him, and at the same time he got to meet my best friend and college housemate who was also visiting from out of town.

After the introductions, it was even harder for us to keep our eyes off one another. We continued to engage in light conversation, oblivious to what was going on around us. We only had eyes for each other, and it was apparent to everyone around us that we were enamored with one another. People were taking notice as the excitement that was going on in our heads and running through our bodies began heating up between the two of us. As we stood waiting for a table, the hostess came over to Terri and me and offered us two chairs at the bar, which we took. I didn't want to leave Dr. Jaeckle, but I knew Terri was hungry, so I told him we were going to the bar. After that I didn't see where he and his family went to sit. Later, I found out that they had been seated at a table in the back of the restaurant, in another room not visible from the bar area.

Terri and I sat comfortably on our bar chairs and ordered a bottle of wine, fresh shrimp, steamed mussels, and a salad. About twenty minutes into our meal, I felt a tap on my shoulder from behind me; I turned around and there he was: my Romeo was standing right in front of me. He reached out and gave me his business card from the

Mayo Clinic. I found it endearing because he immediately flipped the card over to reveal his cell phone number on the back of the card scribbled in blue ink.

"What are you giving this to me for?" I asked, tilting my head and giving him a girlish grin.

He smiled back at me with a boyish grin and said, "It's my cell phone number so you can call or text me."

I laughed, giving him a flirty smile. "Why would I call or text you?" I tilted my head more softly to the side this time. I wondered why he was asking me to contact him: was he afraid to call or text me? Was he afraid to ask for my number?

"I just thought that we should keep in touch," he said, smiling. He was a little nervous, I could tell, and I liked that.

"That's great, but why would I call or text you?" I smiled back shyly while twirling my hair.

He continued to linger at the bar with Terri and me, as some other people around us engaged in our flirty fun. It was obvious to everyone something was going on between him and me. At this point, Terri must have thought it was time to bring me back to earth, because she nudged me so hard I almost fell off my chair.

She pulled me close and whispered in my ear. "What has gotten into you? Stop twirling your hair and acting like you're sixteen. You're not in high school anymore," she said, shaking her head while rolling her eyes.

Okay, so I was a bit embarrassed when she said that to me, and it brought me down to earth a little. But I couldn't help it! I was smitten with this man, and the wine had kicked in by then. We were obviously relaxed and, despite what Terri said to me, he and I continued to flirt like teenagers that night. We both lost track of time, and eventually I quit embarrassing Terri (or she gave up on trying to settle me down) and just went with the flow. I'm sure the wine chilled her out a bit too! He must have spent at least thirty minutes talking to us and flirting with me before he went back to his table to join his family.

I was so happy that he had left me his cell phone number, yippee! It was hard to let him get away that night, but I knew in my heart that it wouldn't be for long. Terri and I went back to talking and I didn't see him for the rest of the evening. When Terri and I returned home that night, I couldn't sleep; I couldn't stop thinking about him.

Much later, Kurt told me that when he returned to his table to join his dad and sister, they had already finished their meal, ordered and ate their desert, and had paid the bill during the time he was away taking to me. Neither he nor I had had any conception of time that evening. Instead, sparks were flying everywhere, and our souls were dancing.

SEVEN YEARS, NEW BEGINNINGS

It wasn't our time when I met Dr. Jaeckle back in 2004. And it wasn't Nicki's time either, because there wasn't a treatment for her disease then—there still isn't. But Nicki was our Cupid, and God led my daughter and I to Dr. Jaeckle so that our souls could touch and then follow each other, waiting until the time was right. God knew that Kurt and I would be together eventually, but I had to first bury my daughter and grieve before he would let us fall in love. There was no miracle for Nicki, and I wish God had granted her one. Kurt may be a brain doctor, but he isn't God, and although God can work miracles through anyone—especially doctors—at times, He did not give Nicki or me the miracle I prayed for.

But, none of this mattered anymore. It was all in the past, and I didn't want to continue dwelling on the past. Rather, I wanted to concentrate on the future. My daughter wasn't here anymore, but I was. Our time here on earth is short, and I didn't want to waste a minute. I was ready to begin a new life, and I wanted to begin again with Kurt. It was time to ask myself if I could see her doctor through different eyes now. Could I call him Kurt instead of Doctor Jaeckle? Could this be my miracle? I was attracted to him, and I knew that I would have to leave my past behind me to go forward with him. I believed there was a definite reason that we were together at Fish Camp after having met seven years earlier, and under much different circumstances. There was also a reason my best friend Terri was with me that night too. Even before my daughter got sick, Kurt and I must have been destined to be together.

Our connection in the clinic seven years earlier was just a spark between the two of us, but that was all it took for our souls to touch. We weren't aware that it happened at the time. We didn't know that Nicki was the catalyst to our love, but in reality she was our angel.

Life is a balance of progression and development. When Nicki was so sick, there was too much pain and hurt: too much suffering in our lives then. But it was the right time for Kurt and me to experience divine intervention. And, after seven years passed, just long enough for our outward appearance to change enough so that we hardly recognized each other, we met again, still drawn to one another because we were already soul mates. Our souls had touched, and God led us to reunite again.

Love doesn't happen by chance, and I didn't know how things would turn out after our night at Fish Camp, a night filled with infinite possibilities. I knew in my heart and soul that God had predetermined that evening for Kurt and me to meet again, as I knew we were always meant to be together. Our love had continued to blossom even apart from one another; it had simply happened that our souls finally found each other. We were so connected, and the feeling was powerful enough that we had to see each other in person to know who we were. I felt we had encountered each other in another life and that we were just then reuniting. We had obviously met many times in our dreams, and energy was flowing through each of us and, if we had met in another time, it must have been so that we would recognize each other for this time here. This was the start of us living and breathing as one. It was evident that our love was growing out of control.

The following morning after Fish Camp, I sent him a

text. I had to contact him first, because he'd given me his number, but I didn't give him mine. Terri told me not to text him right away—she thought I should wait a week—but I sent him a text anyway: I had already waited what seemed a lifetime to meet the man who was touching my soul.

I wrote, "Seven years, new beginnings." The number seven is symbolic, and is used in the Bible 735 times. Seven is the number of completeness and perfection, both physical and spiritual, and the number seven will always be symbolic to me because of the seven-year separation we had before our love blossomed: it was seven years after my daughter died that Kurt and I came together again. Seven years brought new beginnings and created a whole new life for the two of us. Meeting him under different circumstances than when my daughter was sick gave us the freedom to go forward, something we couldn't have done back then, as when Nicki was battling brain cancer my only concern was for her. I wouldn't have been able to let anything, even Dr. Jaeckle, come between my love and dedication to my daughter. In fact, I could only remember taking her to the Mayo Clinic once to be seen by him, though when Kurt and I talked about it later he told me that he'd seen her in the clinic *five* times. This was evidence enough that my Nicki had consumed me. The unconscious can give both protection and motivation, depending on the circumstances.

Right after I sent Kurt my first text, he immediately texted me back. I don't remember what he said, though I recall it was something subtly sweet. He wrote just enough to let me know that he was enamored with me. After the first few texts between us, things progressed, and soon we were messaging every day. At first our texts were simply informing each other about what we'd been doing the previous seven years of our lives, then moved to catching up and getting to know more about what we did on a day-to-day basis.

As we became more familiar with each other's schedules and explored each other's pasts, then we dove into the future. We started sending romantic poems with sexy pictures attached. Then we added music—love songs—texting into the wee hours of the morning. We couldn't let go. We used our devices to explore our minds through poetry, pictures, and music. For seven months, we stayed in constant contact on our phones, never seeing each other in person or speaking on the phone either. Oddly, I was content with not seeing him during this time. I was enjoying getting to know him through our texting. I think we both knew that we would become physical if we saw each other in person, and I don't believe either of us was ready for that yet. He was my soul mate; he wasn't going away anytime soon. I knew he was mine, and I felt safe with him, trusting him with my heart. I knew that one day we would be together in body, mind, and spirit.

Until then, we wrote love letters filled with dreams of running off together to faraway places. He promised me that he would love, honor, and protect me. We filled each other up at a time when we both needed love, acceptance, and companionship, things that neither of us had felt from anyone in a very long time. It was like we had both been starving for love, and now were feeding each other.

During the time when we were texting, we had not asked each other about our belief in God. Then one evening, out of the blue, a message popped up on my iPad. Kurt wrote: I believe in God. I had been waiting for that, but hadn't wanted to ask him. So when I saw his text, I knew God was letting me know that this was the man I would marry. He chose Kurt for me. I truly felt in my heart that God predetermined our love and brought Kurt to me, and because it was eternal, given by God, our love would never end.

TRUST

Several more months passed and I continued to fall deeper in love with Kurt while we were still only texting. But then there came a time when I asked myself, why am I doing this? He lived only two miles away from where I lived, and yet he had never asked me to meet him in person, nor did he ask me out. Even though I had invited him over to my house he never accepted my invitation. That was okay with me then, as I thought that maybe he was in another relationship, one that wasn't going anywhere, and he needed time to end it. That seemed reasonable: it takes time to end relationships, like the one I was in shortly after Nicki died. I found companionship with a man, but not love, and it was hard to end that relationship because he was someone to spend time with. He was a nice man who I respected, and at the time I didn't want him to know that I didn't love him and would never marry him, as it's a selfish thing to do when you're with someone just for their company yet they think you're building a future together. I was lonely, and he felt safe. It's complicated when two people are together for different reasons, especially when one is not in love with the other, and this is what happened to me.

But I knew it was different with Kurt: we were madly in love and I couldn't wait to get my hands on him. Since being with the right person is so important, and I knew that any relationship takes time to figure out, I was patient with him and I gave him the time he needed. I had gone through so many difficult life changes before I connected with Kurt, first with Nicki and then with my husband and the divorce, and I didn't want to rush anything. Even though it was taking what seemed to be a lifetime of waiting for him, I knew it was worth it. It was fate, God working in our lives: it was simply meant to be.

I do think some of my deep emotion for Kurt is because he saw the cancer inside my daughter's brain, and he tried to treat the deadly tumor. He touched her and cared for her during her last year on this earth, and at a time when my husband wasn't there for me, *he* was there for us. He was taking care of my sick daughter, and that meant something, even though he couldn't stop cancer from killing her. He used everything that he had available to save her life, though it was to no avail. He supported me through her suffering more than my husband did at the time. No one could save my Nicki. It's comforting to know that she is safe with God now.

The longer I communicated with Kurt, the deeper I cared for him, and through caring for him I came to know myself better. Kurt was the man that I had been waiting for all my life. As more time passed, our relationship continued to grow even deeper as our love manifested through our souls and inside our hearts. The strong sense of peace and love that I felt in my heart for Kurt was something I had never experienced before, certainly not this way. I was satisfied, comfortable, and I hoped this feeling would last forever.

Only a few select friends of mine knew that we were texting each other and falling in love. I kept it very private, not wanting anyone to judge us. I told Lorrie, one of my closest friends, because I tell her everything. She was by my side when Nicki was sick, and she comforted me when Nicki died; she was so helpful and supportive. Lorrie is a woman who never passes judgment on anyone: she has never passed judgment on Kurt or me, as she accepts me unconditionally and has for over twenty-five years. Whenever I asked her for advice she always gave me the same answer: "Follow your heart." Lorrie knew that I was in love with Kurt, and she knew he was a good man.

I know that nothing in life is for sure. I learned that from watching my daughter battle cancer for almost four years. If it didn't work out between Kurt and I, then I would celebrate the time we had and be thankful that I had a great ride with someone I felt so much emotion and desire for. God provided Kurt at a time when I needed someone sensitive and caring. Something my husband was not. I fell in love with Kurt. People fall in and out of love every day, but if two people are right for each other, they will last an eternity. Love is different when you find your soul mate. I know because I was married but only found my soul mate after my husband left. Moving forward with Kurt was a blessing, and I was unafraid during every step of the way. My faith is always in God. Even though our bodies had not physically touched, our souls had, even before I knew who he was. Neither of us could, or would, ever deny that. We both experienced the spirit of love through God, and it felt amazing. God worked through me, and my faith grew stronger than ever during the time we spent together texting.

Some people don't feel safe following their hearts, others are afraid of taking risks. They might be afraid of failure or of getting hurt. I was not afraid. I had learned how to release my inhibitions and not to live in fear. After losing Nicki to a horrible disease, hidden inside her head for years, I learned that anything can happen to anyone at any time, good or bad. We don't get to choose the things that happen to us. God lives in my heart, and therefore I felt assured that Kurt was part of God's plan for my life. I felt completely safe and secure with the choice I made. I put my faith and trust in God, and did not fear the outcome.

2013

Time continues on with or without us here. It's been eight years since my daughter Nicki died. Kurt proposed to me on October 8, 2013, in a cabin called "Dreams Come True" in Pigeon Forge, Tennessee, as we stood in front of a romantic fire, staring into one another's eyes, just like we did in Fish Camp. He opened a little blue box that held my diamond ring. It sparkled like the brightest star in the sky. I cried tears of joy. I had waited for this moment for so long.

I will never forget how he gently touched my face with his hand while looking into my eyes and said, "Will you marry me, Bunny?"

I said, "Yes!"

God brought us together and slowly, over time, he developed a deep bond and commitment between the two of us. The first time that I saw Kurt in the clinic with my daughter nine years earlier, I'd had no idea that we would spend the rest of our lives together. But life is unpredictable: when I think back to when Nicki was battling brain cancer, I would never have thought that my husband of twenty-four years, her father, would walk out and file for divorce while our daughter was dying. And I didn't think that I would survive losing either Nicki or my marriage, especially not both at the same time. But neither did I know that God would eventually bring Kurt into my life.

I believe that Kurt was Nicki's gift to me, and she was our Cupid. I wish that I could have given both my kids the gift of having parents that stayed together forever, but I had no control over their father walking out and ending our marriage—anyone can walk out of our life at any time. The best gift I gave to my two kids was being a stay-at-home mom while they were growing up. I tried the best I could to be a good wife and mother, and gave both of my kids all my time and effort for twenty-one years. I know that I made a lot of mistakes as a mom, and if I could take the mistakes back I would. "I'm sorry" is a powerful statement, and I hope my kids know that I'm sorry for all the mistakes I made over the years.

I love both kids with all my heart and soul, not just because they are my kids, but because they gave so much love and respect to me while they were growing up. They both worked hard and got excellent grades in school; they achieved awards and honors beyond what was expected of them. Both Jesse and Nicki had a passion for the performing arts and they pursued their passions with vigor, passions that came from inside them. It was completely their decision to both attend a performing arts high school together; they were always very close. It was sad that Nicki was never given the chance to move to New York City to pursue her ultimate dream of performing on Broadway. But anything is possible, Nicki: and I will try my hardest to get your story out in the world so that one day your dream will come true. I hope and pray that your story and your talent will be seen and come alive on a Broadway stage in New York City.

Jesse now lives in Brooklyn, and Nicki now lives in Heaven, where she is more powerful than she could have ever been on this earth. I now have my dream man, my soul mate. Moving forward, I know that my soul was always connected to Kurt. He was always my destiny, and perhaps my husband walked out so that Kurt and I could be together. This is the force of the universe and the essence of life.

After everyone in my life moved on and I found myself alone, I searched internally, and there I found peace. Through meditation and prayer, I put my trust in God; and, believing in my dreams, I found that dreams really do come true. I thank God every day for bringing the man of my dreams into my life: my knight in shining armor, my hero, my soul mate. When Kurt and I die, and leave our earthly bodies, we will find each other again, and I will reunite with my Nicki, and we will never be separated. Eternal life is the greatest gift of all from God. It is the ultimate promise.

TEN YEARS LATER

2015

Ten years have passed since I last saw my daughter's pretty blue eyes. Every day I miss her, and long to kiss her and hold her in my arms. I want to sit and talk to her. I want to hear her laughter. I want to wipe all her tears away. In my heart, I know these things have been resolved in Heaven, but I still long to hold her in my arms again here on earth. I promised her I would be all right. And God promised me that I would see her again, and I will. There have been so many promises, and I know that these things will happen. Believing is the key to one day seeing.

God has blessed me in so many ways. My son, Jesse, continues to make me proud; finding my soul mate Kurt was a beautiful gift from God. Peace and quiet remain a big part of my life. My writing keeps my mind active and alive. When Nicki was here, and even after she was gone, she's still teaching me how to survive and how to persevere through hard times. She taught me how to endure and how to trust. Though God gave her to me for nineteen years, I wanted more time. I had hoped to be able to do all the things that mothers and daughters do together until I was gone. I wanted to be the mother of the bride; I wanted to hold her grandchildren. I hold these hopes and dreams in my heart, and have expressed these feelings many times in books and journals. I wish she were still here, and that I wasn't just writing all this in a book. But it didn't work out that way: we can't predict life.

Nicki was a good, kind person, and she possessed a

gentle heart. Her spirit is still all around those who knew and loved her. Nicki made me a better person. I believe one day her lost future will make sense. A wise person once said, "It's not how you start, it's how you finish." Nicki finished very well.

Kurt and Jesse are the loves of my life. They are both strong, courageous men. Jesse had to watch his sister die; he held his hand over her heart until the last beat. He is now an only child. Nicki would be so proud of her brother as she saw him earn a full scholarship to college and graduated *summa cum laude*. He's also a black belt in Brazilian Jiu-Jitsu, and has many international medals. He's an amazing guitarist. He lives in Brooklyn pursuing his dreams, and has many future goals ahead. I'm so very proud of my son.

Life is a series of comings and goings, hellos and goodbyes. There are things we have no control over, like how long our life will be, or who will stay and who will walk away. We can only make our own choices in life, and I hope we all choose to be kind and honest. I hope we all try harder and love deeper, and accept what we have no control over. We can make a choice to be happy no matter the circumstances.

That night in the cabin, Kurt and I created a dream, making the choice to go forward together to nourish and grow our love. "Our dreams are what keep us moving forward," he said. I smiled!

TWELVE YEARS LATER

MAY 14, 2017: MOTHERS DAY

Kurt and I were married at Cornman Farms in Dexter, Michigan, on Mother's Day 2017.

I wore a beautiful white satin-and-lace wedding dress with a long train. My sister Lynn was my maid of honor, and my son Jesse walked me arm-in-arm down the aisle to my husband Kurt. My grand-nephew Jayce was our ring bearer, and my grand-niece Jade was our flower girl. Kurt's daughter Joanna was our bridesmaid, and Kurt's ninety-two-year-old father was his best man. My mom, Beverly Coleman, was right beside me, beaming as mother of the bride. Sadly, she now has dementia, but I was thankful that she enjoyed the wedding and that she still knows that I'm her daughter. It was a wonderful gift to have both Kurt's dad and my mom at our wedding.

CLOSING THOUGHTS

2017

Mike and I started out happy and excited to begin our lives together. We met in 1981 when he was a senior at the University of Michigan. He was an All-American, and captain of the men's tennis team; I was working as a hairdresser at a salon on campus. He was twenty-one, while I was twenty-seven. We were already married by 1982, when he won the NCAA tennis tournament that May. He was the first—and only—married champion in NCAA history. Our son Jesse was born the following year in November 1983, and Nicki was born October 3, 1985. After winning the NCAA tournament, Mike was given wildcards into the four grand slam tournaments: the Australian, French, Wimbledon, and US Open. He had to qualify to get into the other tournaments during the first year, until he obtained a high enough ranking to get into the main draws.

The first five years of our marriage were spent primarily traveling abroad and throughout North America with our two kids while Mike competed in tournaments to earn a living for our family. I remember our marriage being the happiest after Jesse was born. We were both so happy together, and Mike was a good father. He always played with the kids and taught them sports, especially tennis: both kids had tennis rackets in their hands by two years old! When Mike retired from the ATP tour at twenty-seven, he moved us to Ponte Vedra Beach, and took the job at the Inn and Club, we enjoyed all the amenities together as a family—and those were good times. The best times of our marriage, when I believe we were happiest, was when the kids were young, before middle school. Things only began to change a few years before Nicki got sick, when there were signs of changes in her before doctors eventually found the tumor.

Even fourteen years after my daughter's death and my divorce, I still haven't found the answers to how it all happened. And I don't believe in going back: I have accepted what I don't understand. Grieving is such a complicated process that even years down the road it's still hard to make sense of how Nicki's father left at the worst possible time in our lives. Sometimes I wonder in what ways my daughter's death changed the course of my life. I do think her diagnosis put Mike over the top. But I wonder if I would I still be married to her father had she not gotten the brain tumor and died. Research shows that parents who lose a child have an 80 percent chance of divorcing; could the stress and shock of her death have been the cause of our divorce? I hope not: one would think that losing a child would bond both parents' love and commitment to each other.

But it doesn't work that way—at least for us it didn't. I was the one who wanted our marriage to survive, but I think Mike knew that all my attention and energy was going to Nicki and not to our marriage. I felt that we had already invested a lot of time and effort into our marriage over the years and that we could survive. After all, we were losing Nicki. I didn't want to lose our marriage too, or the future we could have had together with our son if Mike had stayed.

The reality was that Nicki's death did not bring us closer together—quite the opposite. But what if Nicki's cancer had nothing to do with the downfall of our marriage? Maybe our marriage was dying way before she got sick. I don't know this for sure, but I do know that while she battled cancer my mind was completely on her. Everything in my life had to do with her health, her treatments, her medicines, and her surgeries, all the things that consumed my day-to-day life for three years until she died. Maybe it was *me* who eventually gave up on our marriage. I remember a time when Mike tried to bring us closer, but I was so busy with the kids then, putting all my energy into raising them.

It's very foggy now as I try to think back and make sense of all that happened to our family. Twenty-five years is a long time to be married to a person, and the three years we watched our daughter battle cancer seemed like an eternity. And then to lose her was devastating. Nicki's disease, and watching her suffer, was a huge strain on our marriage. Her cancer changed everything in our lives.

Something sticks out in my mind that happened when Nicki first got diagnosed. She was having surgery to remove the tumor; or rather, the doctors were going to remove as much of the tumor as they could without causing her to go blind or lose her speech. During the surgery, Mike and I sat outside the operating room on the floor, side by side, backs up against the wall, our legs stretched out in front of us, waiting for Nicki's surgery to be over. He was stone cold and didn't talk to me at all during this time. It was awkward and cold in the hallway, and I was scared.

I turned to look at him and said, "We're bound together now. We have to stay together forever, for each other and for Jesse and Nicki." He didn't look at me or make eye contact when I said that. He just stared straight ahead at the wall, never blinking an eye. I knew then that he had checked out, and I wondered then how I was going to do this on my own. I think that is the moment in time when I knew that Mike couldn't handle it, and he had already drawn away from me.

After that day, while Nicki was recovering from her surgery, Mike became more and more withdrawn, and I found myself begging him to stay with us. He finally announced to the three of us that he was leaving. Nicki begged him to stay, crying and pleading with him not to go, but he had already made his decision: he was moving out. I don't know what had happened to him, or how he could leave while his daughter was dying. But he did. After he moved out, I drove Nicki over to see him whenever she wanted to go. Eventually there came a time when it got too hard for her to walk up the steps to his condo, and she didn't want to go anymore.

Mike moved out January 1; Nicki died April 29; we were divorced that December, six months later. I wish he had stayed until Nicki passed. We knew that she was going to die—the doctors told us the truth, and Nicki knew too. I believe it would have been better for Nicki if he had stayed, since it caused her a lot of worry and stress. I don't think any kids are happy to see their parents get divorced, let alone when that child is dying.

After Nicki died, while I was living alone, I came to realize that the divorce was the best thing for me. I just didn't like the timing. Mike had never given any explanation as to why he wanted a divorce, and of course I sometimes wonder if he had a girlfriend, or had been cheating on me. But I don't know that. Many of the things that happened to us spun out of control and changed the course we were on. It was especially hard not knowing what would happen to our daughter, since even though the doctors had told us she would not survive a glioblastoma, we still remained hopeful. That is why we must trust in God, because He has a purpose for all pain and suffering.

Jesse and I are still very close, but we don't talk much about his relationship with his father, though if he wants to I will listen. We have had other extended family members who have passed since Nicki's death, but our divorce caused some estrangement on his side of the family for me. It's sad because I love Mike's father and mother, as well as his siblings, and I lost a lot of family on his side when we divorced. But I've had closure since then and I'm okay. I still have a lot of family on my side, and we are very close. I think we have all moved on with our lives.

What I have learned from the experience of watching my daughter die a horrible death is to never give up hope. We can't live on this earth, with human bodies, without experiencing both joy and pain. Maybe at some point in time the reason for Nicki's suffering and her untimely death will be revealed. And if not in this lifetime, I will know the reason on the day when I see Nicki's face and hold her in my arms again.

Life is ever-changing, and during the past fourteen years a lot has changed in my life. But some things remain the same: my daily walks long along the Atlantic Ocean where I have collected hundreds of olive shells—I call them "brain shells." I enjoy daily rituals of meditation and prayer. I still collect shiny pennies that I find on the pavement, in parking lots, and on sidewalks; I've collected handfuls of pennies, and keep them in a special box. I still stretch out over my king-size bed to pray, and at times to cry, but not as much as I used to. Life has been kind enough to soften the blow a little more each year, but crying still feels pretty healing at times.

I've learned to stop constantly asking God *why*? I just about wore myself out doing that. And even though I think about Nicki every day, I do know that grieving, while never disappearing completely, will subside with time. Grieving comes in waves, just like the ocean washing over me, carrying me, twisting and tossing me until the waves calm and turn into ripples. I pray for patience and forgiveness toward others who have hurt or offended me during this painful journey. I pray that others will forgive me when I hurt them. I hope I can trust again. It is a struggle at times: I desire a quiet life, a life of peace and much less sorrow— but don't we all? The journey that I took with my daughter weakened me somewhat, but it also strengthened me, making me wiser in so many ways. Grieving is a long, tedious road that many are on at one time or another in life. Some walk it forever. If it were not for my love of writing, I don't know how I would continue to heal from my daughter's death. Writing is the outlet for my passion and my pain.

Until the time comes when God calls me home and I take my last breath, I will continue to move forward, always putting my trust in God. I will do all that I can do to live a full, happy, healthy life because I know that one day I will be united with my daughter again. On that day, all my hurts will be gone, and I will hold her so tight. I will never let her go. Until that day, I forgive all, and I hope that all will forgive me. I chose love.

CREDITS

Oil Portraits: Original Sacred Artwork, by Ellen Jones
www.Joypeace3art.com
Ten percent of all portrait commissions go to the Nicki Leach Foundation

Terri Devall – Devall Design, Ltd.
www.Terridevalldesign.com

Author photo and photo of Kurt and Bunny walking on the beach, by Stacy Dellone Photography
www.stacydellonephotography.com

www.bunnyleach.com

Nicki Leach

FOUNDATION

"Don't frown because it's over...
smile because it happened."

www.nickileach.org

Helping Adolescents and Young Adults with cancer
pursue their educational dreams and goals

The mission of the Nicki Leach Foundation, a nonprofit organization, is to provide modest financial assistance to young adults, aged sixteen to thirty-nine, afflicted with cancer. We focus on this particular age group as it includes the highest number of underinsured individuals in the US, many of whom are often caught between completing their education and actual employment with insurance benefits. Most have already exhausted their financial resources and, given their diagnoses and disabilities, have significant trouble finding jobs. The foundation also provides funding for glioblastoma research in adolescents and young adults.

One year after Nicki's passing, the Nicki Leach Foundation established an endowment at the University of North Florida in her memory. The Nicki Leach Foundation Endowed Scholarship is available for students who have cancer. Ours is the first of its kind at the university. Nicki would be so proud to know that other young women and men like her, experiencing the same hardships from cancer as she had, will now be given the chance to continue their education during the fight of their lives.

Nicki Leach Foundation
www.nickileach.org

ABOUT ATMOSPHERE PRESS

Atmosphere Press is an independent full-service publisher for books in genres ranging from non-fiction to fiction to poetry, with a special emphasis on being an author-friendly approach to the challenges of getting a book into the world. Learn more about what we do at atmospherepress.com.

We encourage you to check out some of Atmosphere's latest releases, which are available at Amazon.com, BarnesandNoble.com, and via order from your local bookstore:

Letting Nicki Go, nonfiction by Bunny Leach

Mandated Happiness, a novel by Clayton Tucker

Spots Before Stripes, a novel by Jonathan Kumar

Leaving the Ladder, nonfiction by Lynda Bayada

Let the Little Birds Sing, a novel by Sandra Fox Murphy

They are Almost Invisible, poems by Elizabeth Carmer

Love Your Vibe, nonfiction by Matt Omo

Transcendence, poems and images by Vincent Bahar Towliat

Gone Fishing, children's fiction by Carmen Petro

Time Do Not Stop, poems by William Guest

Adrift, poems by Kristy Peloquin

Dear Old Dogs, a novella by Gwen Head

Owlfred the Owl Learns to Fly, a picture book by Caleb Foster

Bello the Cello, a picture book by Dennis Mathew

Ghost Sentence, poems by Mary Flanagan

Winter Park, a novel by Graham Guest

That Scarlett Bacon, a picture book by Mark Johnson

Makani and the Tiki Mikis, a picture book by Kosta Gregory

What Outlives Us, poems by Larry Levy

How Not to Sell, nonfiction by Rashad Daoudi

That Beautiful Season, a novel by Sandra Fox Murphy

What I Cannot Abandon, poems by William Guest

Surviving Mother, a novella by Gwen Head

All the Dead Are Holy, poems by Larry Levy

Rescripting the Workplace, nonfiction by Pam Boyd

Such a Nice Girl, a novel by Carol St. John

ABOUT BUNNY LEACH

Bunny Leach's background is rich in variety, giving her a distinct authorial advantage in creating the heart-wrenching and reflective memoir and self-help book *Letting Nicki Go: A Mother's Journey through Her Daughter's Cancer*, and now its follow-up, *Breathing New Life*. Seamlessly blending her history and experiences during her daughter's battle with cancer with keen introspective meditations on faith and lessons about grief and healing, Leach uses her life story with wit and grace to offer the reader a redemptive experience of their own.

Born in Michigan, Bunny left the state after an early marriage to her first husband, a rising star on the Association of Tennis Professionals ATP tour, traveling widely and living abroad with her spouse and subsequently their two small children. Bunny developed her observational skills as a temporary ex-pat and young mother, as well as the start of a journaling habit that would serve her well throughout the years. Upon returning to the States, the family settled in Florida, where Bunny took on full-time responsibilities as a homemaker and mother, diving into community life and using her spare time to further her interests in writing and home design.

After her teenage daughter's death from cancer, Bunny returned to college at the University of North Florida and, after studying a course direction in psychology, she became a certified life coach helping people find the answers that lie within themselves so that they may achieve their dreams and goals. Additionally, after a successful one-woman renovation of her beloved beach home in Florida, Bunny began work in home staging and redesign, and is pleased to offer her services to individuals and realtors alike.

Before her daughter died, Nicki asked her mother if she would do something to help others who are suffering with cancer like she was. In Nicki's memory Bunny began the Nicki Leach Foundation, a non-profit organization providing education scholarships and funding for cancer research on AYA tumors (Adolescence and Young Adults), age 15-39. As the founder and CEO of the foundation, Bunny plays an integral role in ensuring that her daughter's memory is kept alive through constant generosity and meaningful action, providing the material means to further the dreams and goals of other young people afflicted with cancer.

Bunny also began volunteering her time and efforts as a Patient Advocate working with the American Society of Clinical Oncology ASCO.org, and is a member of the Molecular Tumor board for TAPUR, the Targeted Agent Profiling Utilization Registry (tapur.org). She is on the patient advocate committee for the Alliance (alliance forclinicaltrialsinoncology.org), which is supported by the NCI National Cancer Institute.

Bunny lives in Ponte Vedra Beach, Florida, enjoying the beauty of the ocean and her daily walks and meditation, which is so important for her. She is writing a new nonfiction book, *Mourning Mothers*, and a novel, *Once A Week*. The prequel to *Breathing New Life: Finding Happiness after Tragedy*, called *Letting Nicki Go: A Mother's Journey through Her Daughter's Cancer*, is also available from Atmosphere Press and can be purchased online.